D1433520

FA

WATER GARDEN PLANTS

WATER GARDEN PLANTS

The Complete Guide

David Case

The Crowood Press

First published in 1991 by
The Crowood Press Ltd
Ramsbury, Marlborough
Wiltshire SN8 2HR

British Library Cataloguing in Publication Data

Case, David
Water garden plants.
1. Water gardens
I. Title
635.9674

ISBN 1 85223 411 3

Picture credits

All line-drawings are by Jan Sparrow.

Typeset by Hope Services (Abingdon) Ltd
Printed in Great Britain by
Redwood Press Ltd, Melksham, Wilts

CONTENTS

ACKNOWLEDGEMENTS

I am grateful to many people who have helped me in different ways. Their constructive ideas and suggestions have enabled me to write this book.

I am indebted to Mr J. Lockwood, a friend of long standing and Horticultural Officer to Poole Borough Council, England who read through the original manuscript and made valuable suggestions. To Mr N. H. Bennett, who kindly helped me through the listings of the water lilies and for allowing me the privilege of collecting photographic material from his unrivalled collection at his nursery at Chickerell, Weymouth, England.

My thanks to Mr P. Hickman, Mr T. Mason and Mr C. K. Thornton for allowing me to collect photographic material from their delightful gardens, and to Mrs J. Davis for her patience and accurate typing and for coping with so many Latin names.

INTRODUCTION

When I was first approached to write a book on water garden plants, my initial reaction was that there were already plenty of excellent books on the subject and that another one would be either a duplication or one that could be controversial. It was then explained to me that what was wanted was a book to cover a wide range of plants, with details of their care and cultivation and their place in the water garden.

Most water garden books are written for the benefit of the amateur gardener and give guidance and instruction in the siting of a water garden and the selection of a modest collection of plants suitable for such a feature. In spite of the fact that most of the past twenty-five years of my life has been spent growing water lilies and aquatic plants, the task of writing this book has demonstrated conclusively to me what tremendous scope there is for creating a water garden in which to grow a wide range of aquatic plants and waterside perennials.

A water garden need not be large: a tub or half-barrel are once again becoming popular for creating a water garden in miniature, particularly where space is limited. Where there is a large expanse of water the possibilities are endless.

My task has made me much more aware of how parochial the United Kingdom is towards the range of aquatic and allied plants available from the main nursery stock outlets, the ubiquitous garden centres. Fortunately, though, this trend is now in reverse. With more time for leisure activities, and with gardening taking a high priority, many owners of large gardens or estates are opening them to the public. (The National Gardens Scheme's *Yellow Book* will bear this out.) These gardens can offer a lot in the way of plants, many of which are raised and sold by their owners in order to finance high maintenance costs. As a result, increasing numbers of amateur growers have turned professional by incorporating a small nursery or plant centre within their garden or estate. This has been encouraged by that excellent publication *The Plantfinder*. In this you will find an unrivalled range of nursery stock available from small family-run enterprises – stock that garden centres generally no longer sell. This new band of enthusiastic amateurs-turned-professional often show a knowledge of nomenclature that is quite exceptional.

Another valuable aid to the keen amateur and professional in the United Kingdom is the formation of the National Council for the Conservation of Plants and Gardens (NCCPG), founded in 1979. It has been an enormous success. The membership of over 5,000 is divided into counties and their activities include locating and surveying old and important gardens and plant collections. Most groups hold annual or twice-yearly plant sales – an important outlet for the small specialist nursery as well as a source of inspiration for the keen amateur looking for plants for special purposes.

It is a little disconcerting, however, that aquatic plants are not more widely shown at any of the major flower shows. In the 1920s and 1930s Perrys of Enfield staged outstanding exhibits of water lilies and aquatics at the Southport Flower Show and the Royal Horticultural Society Westminster Flower Shows. Their Gold Medal Chelsea exhibits of the 1950s and 1960s were unsurpassed. To date no one has come anywhere near to emulating their unique displays.

Within this book you will find descriptive listings of a comprehensive range of aquatic and waterside perennials, their methods of propagation and cultural methods, including a number of practical suggestions for planting schemes for large and small water gardens. It will be noticed that with some genera the nomenclature will differ from other books. This is because the botanists are at odds and cannot agree on a universally accepted name. I have stayed with the well-known and generally accepted names, and give any new or alternative names in brackets.

The aim of this book is to encourage the keen amateur and professional alike to become familiar with the wide range of water plants in cultivation and to develop the practical knowledge required to create a delightful addition to our gardens and landscaped areas.

1
THE HARDY WATER LILIES AND DEEP-WATER AQUATICS

THE WATER LILIES, NYMPHAEA (ORDER NYMPHAEACEAE)

This genus comprises over fifty species, including the handsome tropical and hardy species which have rhizomatous or tuberous rootstocks. They are distributed throughout the northern hemisphere and in the tropical regions of the world, but are singularly absent in New Zealand. For this book I shall stay exclusively with the hardy species and varieties.

The use of water as a feature in gardens is exceedingly old, particularly so in southern Europe and in the Far Eastern countries. Theophrastus describes a number of aquatic plants that were seen in Europe and it is known that the Romans featured pools, mostly formal, in their gardens. In the United Kingdom, however, it was not until the early 1700s that water as a feature became an accepted form of landscape gardening. William Kent led the way with gardens like Stowe in Buckinghamshire and he influenced Henry Hoare's architects in designing the Stourhead landscape in Wiltshire. Lancelot 'Capability' Brown soon followed with such notable gardens as Blenheim and Sheffield Park in Sussex. (The water lilies came much later.)

The only lily that is native to the United Kingdom is the white water lily, *Nymphaea alba*, the glory of the lake, which is also widespread throughout the waterways of Europe. In the United Kingdom, however, in many of its former habitats this lily is no longer in existence. From the Victorian times, when water gardening became increasingly popular, this native was continually being dug up from the rivers and replanted in pools in private gardens.

The first country estate to cultivate aquatic plants in a heated conservatory was Chatsworth, the home of the 1st Duke of Devonshire, whose head gardener was Sir Joseph Paxton. He was successful in growing and producing flowering plants of *Victoria regia*. *Nymphaea candidissima* is reputed also to have been grown and to have flowered well under glass at Chatsworth.

In 1856 a variety of *Nymphaea alba*, *N. alba* 'Rubra', was discovered growing in a lake in the north-west of Oster Gothland, Sweden. According to M. Froebel, this plant comes true from seed. It is a beautiful lily which succeeds best in cold water. On opening, the flowers are a rosy-pink, turning to red with age. It was not until 1878 that this lily was introduced into England. Since then it has been given numerous names – *N. alba* variety 'Rosea', *N. sphaerocarpa* variety 'Rubra' and *N. caspery*. It is now very doubtful whether it can be obtained from any British nursery. In 1786 an American species was introduced into England, the sweet-smelling white *Nymphaea odorata*, and about thirty years later a miniature form of *N. odorata* arrived in the United Kingdom, also from America, *N. odorata* variety 'Minor', sometimes known as the millpond lily. The same time saw the arrival of *N. tetragona*, sometimes quoted as being synonymous with *N. pygmaea alba*, though some authorities believe them to be two distinct species, the former being much smaller both in flower and leaf. We are not completely sure where this lily comes from, since it is distributed throughout China and North America. Next to come, in 1812, was *N. odorata* variety 'Rosea', known as the pink Cape Cod water lily. To put yellow into the hardy lilies and those in varying shades of copper and bronze it is assumed that the doubtfully hardy *N. flava* (*N. mexicana*) was used. These comparatively few hardy or near-hardy species from throughout the world were to become parents to many of the most beautiful hardy water lilies in cultivation today.

This was some fifty years or so later, when a Frenchman, M. Joseph Bory Latour-Marliac, gave up an academic career at Paris University to return to manage his parents' estate in the small village of Temple-sur-Lot in the south of France. The district is renowned for its commercial production of market garden crops and fruit trees. We are told through the magazine *The Garden* in 1894 that part of the estate included some 2½ acres (1 hectare) set aside for the propagation and production of bamboos, aquatic plants and water lilies. Within this small section was a good supply of warm water, emerging from numerous springs throughout the year. The water was directed into about forty ponds. These in turn formed streams and many smaller ponds, which were used for cultivating a wide range of aquatic plants and water lilies, with the bamboos serving as screens. By this time Latour-Marliac was very much the professional nurseryman, sending plants to various destinations throughout the world.

Some time after leaving Paris, Marliac came across an important article by Professor Lévêque on tropical water lilies which were growing in pools in the Museum of Natural History. This led him to grow and subsequently to hybridize a number of lilies as an amateur. Soon he turned professional and raised his hybrids commercially. One of his first major introductions was *N.* × *marliacea* 'Chromatella' (the well-known yellow variety), raised in 1877 with one of the parents being *Nymphaea flava* (*N. mexicana*). This was followed by that exquisite miniature *N. pygmaea* 'Helvola' in 1879. The same year saw *N. odorata* 'Sulphurea', a hybrid between *N. odorata* and *N. flava* (*N. mexicana*). In 1880 came *N.* × *marliacea* 'Albida', and *N.* × *marliacea* 'Carnea' followed in 1887. These then were the forerunners of over eighty varieties which were to come during the next thirty years or so. All varied in colour, shape and vigour, to suit most sizes of lakes and ponds.

One of the first gardens in England to accommodate these early hybrids from France – in 1880 – was the Cambridge Botanic Garden. Here a natural water garden was constructed with puddled clay, to make it watertight. The water lilies were planted in mounds of soil placed below water level in the middle of the lake.

William Robinson, of the famous garden at Gravetye Manor, details the planting of the early hybrids in his book *The English Flower Garden*. A once important London garden is also described as having about a dozen species and varieties including the British native *N. alba* and *N. alba* 'Rubra' which were established in about 1890. In 1894 a further twelve varieties were planted. It is interesting to note from his book that the dozen small tubers arrived in one parcel by post from M. Latour-Marliac Nursery. How long they took to arrive we do not know, but all survived. Robinson and Marliac became such good friends that the eighth edition of *The English Flower Garden* was dedicated to him. Latour-Marliac was acclaimed to be a hybridizer extraordinary, producing numerous new varieties almost every year. In 1911 he died and it seems that the secret of his success died with him. Although the business was continued by his daughter and son-in-law, Maurice Laydeker, the rate at which new hybrids became available slowed down considerably, the last being in 1937.

Across the Atlantic in the United States were several successful nurseries producing some outstanding water lilies, notably *N.* 'William Falconer' by Henry Dreer in 1899 and, in the following year, *N.* 'James Brydon'. Also in America, Mrs Fowler, at her nursery in Kenilworth (near Washington DC), introduced the pink hybrid N. 'Rose Arey' in 1913, followed by N. *odorata* 'Pink Opel' and N. *odorata* 'Helen Fowler', both in 1915.

It is a matter of conjecture just how Latour-Marliac attained such a high success rate in raising so many oustanding water lily hybrids within his lifetime. Perhaps he used a complex method of cross-fertilizing flowers, or perhaps he simply let nature take its course, allowing bees and other flying insects to do the work, and then collecting the resulting fertile seed pods, sowing, and raising the seedlings. As the seedlings reached flowering size it would then be a matter of eliminating anything inferior and retaining the best. I have a theory, which I believe I share with one or two others, that climatic conditions may have played an important part in Marliac's work. The weather in the south of France during the summer is on average much warmer and more settled than it is in England, which could be of great significance in pollination.

Frances Perry states in her book *Water Gardening* (1938; revised 1961): 'Out of 159 recorded crosses we made in 1927, only one pod set seed, and the offspring was no better, and indeed, not as good as many of the existing varieties.'

Since most of these varieties were raised some eighty or so years ago, many have become incorrectly named and so often what you buy in a garden centre or what you have ordered from a nursery is not the lily that is described. It is not the supplier's fault; it goes back much further. Mixed or lost labels, casual staff confusing orders in the height of the lifting season, or substituting one variety for another without labelling accordingly – all can lead to confusion in later years. This is why catalogues listing water lilies often give conflicting descriptions of many of the lilies. Some catalogues and books describe the well-known white water lily N. × *marliacea* 'Albida' as having large scented white flowers with green leaves. Others describe the leaves as having a distinctive brown edge. This is the form that I grow, but it is almost scentless. So which is correct? Or is it another variety altogether? Similarly, the variety N. 'Comanche' is often described as small-flowered orange or apricot changing to copper, yet in Marliac's own words (taken from his catalogue published a year after his death) it is described as having large flowers of a coppery ochre-yellow, reticulated and veined with red. For some, these details would not matter, but to the professional it is important that the stock propagated is authentic.

To help professionals and amateurs alike, the International Water Lily Society was formed in 1984 to further the knowledge and the methods of growing water lilies and aquatic plants. It has also embarked on the task of issuing a checklist of all known *Nymphaea* in cultivation. It is endeavouring to establish the authenticity of the lilies according to Latour-Marliac's descriptions.

And so to the future, which on the face of it looks particularly promising. Since Marliac's death in 1911 very few notable hybrids have come to the fore until just recently. The Americans are now foremost in producing a new range of promising varieties or cultivars of water lilies. Some have already made their way to England and should be available from British nurseries in the near future. There is certainly a dynamism and expertise in the American aquatic nursery business which is almost totally lacking in England.

One leading American nurseryman, Perry Slocum, introduced *N.* 'Pink Perfection' over forty years ago and more recently he offers us such varieties as *N.* 'Pearl of the Pool', a deep-pink variety, *N.* 'Red Cap', *N.* 'Red Flare' and *N.* 'Radiant Red'. There are others yet to be evaluated.

Some enthusiastic work has been quietly taking place at Wychwood Carp Farm near Basingstoke in England, where a cross between *N. pygmaea alba* and *N.* 'Rembrandt' has resulted in hybrids known as *N.* 'Ballerina', *N.* 'Regann', *N.* 'Peach Blossom' and *N.* 'Fiesta'. Although none of these is available at present, they are names that should become more familiar when stocks are propagated and become commercially available. However, I am still convinced that Latour-Marliac's hybrids will be extremely hard to match. It is indeed good news that this work is making a significant contribution to the world of aquatic growers.

At the time of writing I have not yet had the privilege of seeing any of these new hybrids, but I am as optimistic as anyone else who is a devotee of the hardy water lilies. One thing that is certain is that nobody should claim to have discovered Marliac's secret, which died with him. To suggest that any modern method of hybridization employed to raise new cultivars might be the same as Marliac's can only be guesswork.

SOME RECOMMENDED VARIETIES OR CULTIVARS

The following hardy water lilies, as their dates of introduction suggest, have stood the test of time for being thoroughly reliable, long-lived and worthy of planting in garden pools and lakes alike.

Most should be available from specialist nurseries and well stocked garden centres which incorporate an aquatic department.

White and Blush Shades

Strong-growing varieties for the larger ponds and lakes requiring water from 1½ft (50cm) up to 3ft (1m) deep. It is often more important to give sufficient surface area to the most vigorous kinds than to stipulate the precise depths. The following would require an area of approximately 25 square feet (2.5 square metres) of water.

Nymphaea alba   The water lily native to Great Britain. The glory of the lake, only suitable for lakes and natural plantings. Pure white flowers with yellow centres. Enormous leaves. Increases fairly rapidly.

N. 'Colossea' (Marliac, 1901)   A vigorous variety producing a succession of enormous blush pink flowers passing to white. Large green leaves and one of the best for deep water.

N. 'Gladstoniana' (Richardson, 1897)   One of the finest lilies in cultivation raised in the United States. It has huge pure-white flowers often up to 10in (25cm) across when established. The dark-green leaves stand well out of the water and have a distinctive rippling effect to the edges when established. Ideal for large ponds and lakes.

N. 'Gloire du Temple-sur-Lot' (Marliac, 1913)   An unusual hybrid which is remarkable for its double flowers very similar to an incurved chrysanthemum. These open as palest pink, passing to creamy white with age. It needs a season or two to establish but then flowers freely all summer.

N. 'Gonnère' 'Crystal White' (Marliac 1914)   Known in America as 'Snowball'. Enormous snow-white double flowers with green sepals and leaves. This and the previous variety are not quite so vigorous as the other kinds in this section.

N. × *marliacea* 'Albida' (Marliac, 1880)   Strong-growing and possibly one of the most widely grown lilies, often in ponds too small for its vigorous growth. It has large upright pure-white fragrant flowers produced in the greatest profusion. The dark-olive-green foliage has a thin brown edge to the leaf which distinguishes this variety from other whites. Early flowering.

N. tuberosa 'Richardsonii' (Richardson 1894)   Vigorous and distinct with large globular pure-white blooms with conspicuous green sepals. Very effective for large ponds and lakes.

N. 'Virginalis' (Marliac, 1910)   A superlative variety which when established has a long flowering season throughout the summer months. Quite distinct from any other. Slightly incurved shell-shaped petals of purest white with pale rose-coloured sepals. Fragrant.

Medium growing varieties for small ponds and fibreglass pools requiring water from 1–1½ft (30–50cm). Surface area of water covered approximately 12–16 square feet (1.1–1.5 square metres).

N. 'Albatros' (Marliac, 1910)   Large milky-white flowers with lanceolate petals, bronzed-green leaves with red undersides. A distinctive lily.
N. 'Caroliniana Nivea' (Marliac, 1893)   A very-large-flowered form of N. odorata ideally suited for small pools. The pure-white flowers are freely produced and are sweetly scented.
N. 'Hermine' (Marliac, 1910)   Medium-sized flowers with long petals. Leaf uniform green with medium-wide open sinus. Underneath of mature leaf green but reddish when young.
N. odorata alba   A delightful North American species. The pure-white fragrant flowers stand above the water level. Circular pale-green leaves.

Small and pygmaea varieties for sinks, tubs and shallow pools requiring water 6–9in (15–23cm) deep and a surface area of 2–3 square feet (60–90 square centimetres).

N. candida   A pretty bohemian species for small pools. Pure-white flowers with green sepals borne on stiff stems standing several inches out of the water.
N. odorata 'Minor' (syn. pumila)   A very small fragrant lily from the north-eastern states of America. Star-shaped snow-white flowers with pale-green foliage.
N. pygmaea alba   Perhaps the smallest-flowered member of this genus. Delightful tiny snow-white flowers not much more than an inch (2.5cm) across are produced in great abundance throughout the summer. Ideal for sinks or tubs. Some protection from severe frosts will be necessary: cover the sink or tub with boards.

Pink, Rose and Salmon Shades

Strong-growing varieties for large ponds and lakes requiring water from 1½ft (50cm) up to 3ft (1m) and a surface area of approximately 25 square feet (2.5 square metres).

N. 'Amabilis' (Marliac, 1921) A beautiful variety of a strong constitution. The exceptionally large stellate flowers are a delicate shade of salmon pink. Very free-flowering. The leaves are dark ruby red when young but mature to olive green.

N. 'Brackleyi Rosea' (pre-1909) A splendid variety with sweetly scented blooms of deep rose which assume paler shades with age. An ideal lily for the larger pond.

N. 'Mme Wilfron Gonnère' (Marliac) Many-petalled cup-shaped flowers with outer petals white flushed deep rose within. Green sepals. The gap in the leaf (sinus) overlaps. An attractive variety.

N. × *marliacea* 'Carnea' (Marliac, 1887) Perhaps the most widely grown pink water lily. Large soft pink flowers with a rosy tinge towards the base of the sepals. An easily grown variety; very free-flowering. Suitable for the larger ponds and lakes.

N. × *marliacea* 'Rosea' (Marliac, 1887) Very similar to the preceding but the flowers are a shade deeper.

N. 'Masàniello' (Marliac, 1908) The large globular flowers stand well out of the water. A delightful shade of deep rose with white sepals. Very free-flowering.

N. 'Mrs Richmond' (Marliac, 1910) Enormous deep-pink flowers, deeper towards the centre; yellow stamens. Vigorous growth.

N. 'Norma Gedye' A beautiful lily recently introduced from Melbourne, Australia. It is perfectly hardy with deep-cerise-pink flowers. Vigorous growth. Only suitable for large ponds.

N. 'Pink Sensation' (Slocum, 1948) An American variety of outstanding merit. Clear pink flowers that often stay open until late in the day. Free-flowering. This is one of the very best varieties. It is easy to grow but not rampant. Leaf is green but bright-red underneath.

Medium-growing varieties for small ponds and prefabricated pools requiring water from 1–1½ft (30–50cm). Surface area of water covered approximately 12–16 square feet (1.1–1.5 square metres).

N. 'Caroliniana Perfecta' (Marliac, 1893) A beautiful variety with large sweetly scented rose-pink flowers. The compact growth and free-flowering habit make it an ideal choice for the small pond.

N. odorata 'Firecrest' An American hybrid with fragrant deep-pink flowers and prominent red-tipped stamens, giving it a unique appearance.

N. × *laydekeri* hybrids Water lilies designated *laydekeri* are a group of superlative hybrids ideally suited for the smaller ponds or for tub culture. They are all of a free-flowering habit. Medium-sized dark-green foliage.

N. × *laydekeri* 'Lilacea' (Marliac)   Very fragrant small flowers produced in great profusion throughout the summer. On opening, the flowers are soft lilac-mauve, passing with age to deep rose.

N. × *laydekeri* 'Rosea' (Marliac, 1903)   This water lily has become quite rare in recent years. Pale rose colour darkening each day with age.

N. *odorata* 'Helen Fowler'   A beautiful variety and one of the finest of the odoratas with star-shaped shell-pink flowers. The fragrant blooms stand above water level. The purplish young leaves become olive-green.

N. *odorata* 'Luciana' (Dreer)   A pretty small-growing lily with medium-sized star-shaped flowers of rich satiny rose which when established stand well out of the water.

N. *odorata* 'Turicensis'   Soft-rose medium-sized flowers. Sweetly scented. Olive-green circular leaves.

N. *odorata* 'William B. Shaw' (Dreer)   Cup-shaped shell-pink flowers with narrow-pointed petals. Like most *odorata* varieties, the flowers stand well out of the water. Sweetly scented.

N. 'Pink Opal' (Fowler, 1915)   A delightful American variety. The flowers are of a deep coral pink. Ideally suited for the small pond.

N. 'Rose Arey' (Fowler, 1913)   Large stellate perfectly shaped flowers of a rich rose pink. Fragrant and very free-flowering.

N. 'Rose Nymph' ('Rosennymphe') (Junge, 1911)   A most beautiful water lily with large open flowers often 6–7in (15–18cm) across of a deep rose-pink shade passing to white with age. They are fragrant and produced in great abundance.

N. 'Somptuosa' (Marliac, 1909)   Large globular almost double flowers of a rich rose pink with clear orange stamens. It occupies little space so it is well suited for the smaller ponds. Very fragrant, and early-flowering.

Amaranth, Crimson and Red Shades

Strong-growing varieties for the larger ponds and lakes requiring water from 1½ft (50cm) up to 3ft (1m) deep and a surface area of approximately 25 square feet (2.5 square metres).

N. 'Attraction' (Marliac, 1910)   The predominating colour of this variety is a deep purplish-crimson flaked white. The petals are also often tipped pure white. It is vigorous and very free-flowering.

N. 'Charles de Meurville' (Marliac, 1931) A very vigorous variety that needs plenty of room. Large wine-red flowers that lie flat on the water surface with enormous green leaves.

N. 'Conqueror' (Marliac, 1910) This hybrid has large flowers with deep-red centres. Outer petals flaked and spotted white. Robust growth and very free-flowering. A little deeper in colour than 'Attraction'.

N. 'Escarboucle' (Marliac, 1909) Remarkable and quite unique, producing enormous flowers of a uniform shade of intense crimson. Vigorous and extremely free-flowering. Possibly the most outstanding red lily in cultivation.

N. 'Gloriosa' (Marliac, 1896) A very distinct hybrid which has large open currant-red flowers often up to 6in (15cm) in diameter. It is free-flowering and fragrant. A very noticeable feature of this lily is that every developed flower has five sepals. A first choice where space is not adequate is 'Escarboucle'.

N. 'James Brydon' (Dreer, 1902) Without doubt one of the most popular and satisfactory water lilies in cultivation today. The large globular-shaped flowers are of a uniform shade of rich rose crimson and sit flat among the open circular purple leaves. Well adapted for the small pool and robust enough for the larger ones as this lily never becomes overcrowded, but useless for tub culture.

N. 'Newton' (Marliac, 1910) This very distinct variety is similar in shape to the tropical *N. stellata*. The large stellate flowers stand well out of the water. These are a brilliant shade of rose vermilion with extra-long orange stamens.

N. 'Picciola' (Marliac, 1913) Very strong-growing, producing enormous crimson flowers. The leaves are sometimes blotched with maroon. Suitable for the larger ponds or lakes.

N. 'René Gérard' (Marliac, 1914) A very popular and adaptable lily for most ponds except for very shallow pools. The large upright star-shaped flowers are of a rich rose streaked crimson towards the centre. Moderate growth and very free-flowering. The distinctive feature of this variety is the very wide sinus in the leaf.

N. 'William Falconer' (Dreer, *c.* 1899) Perhaps the deepest shade among the water lilies. Blood-red flowers contrast vividly with the rich golden anthers, dark-purple foliage. Not so vigorous as the others listed in this section but can be grown in water up to 2ft (60cm) deep.

Medium-growing varieties for small ponds and prefabricated pools requiring water from 1–1½ft (30–50cm). Surface area covered approximately 12–16 square feet (1.1–1.5 square metres).

N. 'Andreana' (Marliac, 1895) This is a variety not often seen. The flowers vary in colour with age from red shaded ochre to yellow, and stand well out of the water. The handsome foliage is variegated with purple.

N. 'Atropurpurea' (Marliac, 1901) One of the best of its colour. It is free-flowering and blood-red. Not dissimilar to 'William Falconer' but the flowers are more open.

N. 'Ellisiana' (Marliac, 1896) Here we have a first-class hybrid. The flowers are a rich vermilion red with orange-red stamens sitting flat on the surface of the water. Plain green leaves. Suitable also for rock garden pools.

N. 'Froebeli (1898) A variety raised in the Munich Botanic Garden by Otto Froebel, and still one of the most commendable. Medium-sized flowers of a rich wine crimson. Dark-olive-green foliage. When established, the flowers are thrust above the surface of the water. An excellent choice for the small pool.

N. × *laydekeri* 'Fulgens' (Marliac, 1895) As already mentioned, all the *laydekeri* hybrids are first-class lilies for shallow pools and tubs. This one is outstanding, with iridescent crimson flowers. The sepals are pinkish-white inside with orange-red stamens. The green leaves are occasionally splashed with maroon.

N. × *laydekeri* 'Purpurata' (Marliac, 1895) Very free-flowering with pale-pink outer petals, crimson centres and stamens of bright orange-red.

N. 'Lucida' (Marliac, 1894) A beautiful variety with large open flowers of a rich rosy vermilion deepening towards the centre. The large leaves are heavily variegated purple. Useless for tub culture.

N. × *marliacea* 'Ignea' (Marliac, 1893) Another hybrid in this section with large flowers but suitable for shallow pools. The flowers are a uniform shade of carmine-red and are freely produced, with fiery red anthers. The bronze leaves turn with age to dark green mottled with brown variegations.

N. 'Sanguinea' (Marliac, 1894) The flowers are a brilliant shade of carmine crimson with olive-green foliage slightly variegated brown. Ideal for the smaller pool.

N. 'Vésuve' (Marliac, 1906) The large open flowers are a brilliant shade of deep amaranth red. Bright-red stamens. Free flowering.

Small variety for rock garden pools and tubs requiring water 9–12in (23–30cm) deep and a surface area of 2–3 square feet (60–90 square centimetres).

N. pygmaea 'Rubra'   The small flowers on opening are lilac-rose, changing to ruby red with age. They are slightly larger in leaf and flower than the other *pygmaea* forms.

Yellow Shades

Strong-growing varieties for large ponds and lakes requiring water from 1½ft (50cm) up to 3ft (1m) deep. Surface area covered approximately 25 square feet (2.5 square metres).

N. 'Colonel A. J. Welch' (Marliac)   Not one of the best yellows but will grow in deeper water than the others in this section. Pale canary-yellow flowers sparsely produced with an abundance of light-green foliage.

N. × *marliacea* 'Chromatella' (Marliac, 1877)   The superb and very well known water lily. Its large primrose-yellow flowers are produced in great profusion. Bold variegated maroon and green foliage.

N. 'Moorei' (Adelaide Botanic Garden, 1900)   Strong canary-yellow flowers with large green foliage spotted purple. Although this variety comes from Australia it is perfectly hardy in cooler climates.

N. 'Sunrise'   Unrivalled among the yellows because of its many very large golden-yellow petals. This water lily is easily recognized by the dark-green leaves with reddish undersides. The stems to both leaves and flowers are pubescent. It is not so vigorous as the other varieties in this section and needs a season to establish, after which it will flower freely.

Small and *pygmaea* varieties for rock garden pools and tubs requiring water 6–9in (15–23cm) deep and surface area of 2–3 square feet (60–90 square centimetres).

N. odorata 'Sulphurea Grandiflora' (Marliac, 1888)   Fragrant sulphur-yellow flowers are large and star-shaped. Attractive foliage blotched reddish-brown. It needs to be planted in full sun and in warm localities to flower well, otherwise it is very disappointing.

N. pygmaea 'Helvola' (Marliac, 1879)   The smallest of all the water lilies and the gem of the genus. The tiny flowers are a soft primrose-yellow. The olive-green leaves are attractively blotched brown above and reddish and spotted beneath. Ideally suited for growing in bowls, tubs and shallow pools.

Copper and Orange Shades

For small ponds and tubs requiring water 1–1½ft (30–45cm) deep
and a surface area of up to 9–15 square feet (0.8–1.4 square metres).
The water lilies in this section are less vigorous and their surface
spread is often less than other varieties in the corresponding
sections. This makes them particularly suitable for small prefabricated
pools.

N. 'Aurora' (Marliac, 1895)   This water lily opens as a pinkish-
yellow changing to reddish-orange and finally to ruby red. Very
pretty foliage mottled and marbled.

N. 'Comanche' (Marliac, 1908)   Large-sized flowers whose inner
petals are coppery yellow shading to scarlet, outer petals pale-
yellow passing to a shade of copper-red. Orange stamens. Olive-
green leaves speckled brown.

N. 'Graziella' (Marliac, 1904)   Very free-flowering medium-sized
flowers of an orange-red shade, greenish petals and reddish sepals.
Olive-green leaves marbled purple. Suitable for tub culture.

N. 'Indiana' (Marliac, 1912)   The colour variation is considerably
marked. The flowers on opening are an orange-yellow, gradually
passing to brilliant copper-red. Mottled foliage and very free-
flowering.

N. 'Paul Hariot' (Marliac, 1905)   A distinctive water lily which
has large clear yellow flowers delicately shaded coppery-red, from
a relatively small growing plant. The undersides of the leaves are
spotted red. Free-flowering.

N. 'Sioux' (Marliac, 1908)   The large flowers on opening are a rich
chrome yellow with the inner petals suffused bronze passing to
deep copper-red with age, a curious but pleasing shade. The
bronzy-green foliage is blotched with dark brown above and
reddish brown on the underside.

N. 'Solfatare' (Marliac, 1906)   The star-shaped flowers of coppery
red stand well out of the water. Very free-flowering. Olive-green
foliage spotted with red underneath.

WATER LILIES AT A GLANCE

Realizing that many gardeners may be bewildered by the numerous
varieties listed I have selected the six most suitable for beginners in
each category. These are generally available from garden centres
which have an aquatic department. For the more adventurous, seek

out the specialist aquatic nurseries where the plants are grown. There you will find a wider range of plants available and expect advice from the grower or his knowledgeable staff. Nurseries may not be so orderly or so immaculately kept as garden centres but their prices are invariably keener.

Six best water lilies for small pools 1–1½ft (30–45cm) deep and each requiring a surface area of 9–12 square feet (0.8–1.1 square metres).

Nymphaea candida	pure white
N. 'Firecrest'	pink with orange stamens
N. × *laydekeri* 'Lilacea'	lilac pink
N. × *laydekeri* 'Fulgens'	deep red
N. 'Ellisiana'	bright red
N. 'Froebeli'	wine red

Six best water lilies for water 1½–2ft (45–60cm) deep and each requiring a surface area of 12–16 square feet (1.1–1.5 square metres).

Nymphaea 'Chromatella'	yellow
N. 'James Brydon'	rich rose crimson
N. 'Hermine'	pure white
N. 'Gloriosa'	currant red
N. 'René Gérard'	deep rose
N. 'Rose Arey'	strong clear pink

Six best water lilies for large ponds and lakes growing in 2–3ft (60cm–1m) water and each requiring a surface area of 25 square feet (2.5 square metres).

Nymphaea 'Brackleyi Rosea'	deep rose
N. 'Gladstoniana'	pure white
N. *Colossea*	blush pink
N. 'Escarboucle'	brilliant crimson
N. *tuberosa* 'Richardsonii'	globular, pure white
N. 'Charles de Meurville'	wine red

DEEP-WATER AQUATICS

Aponogeton (Order Aponogetonaceae)

Aponogeton distachyos (from *apon*, Celtic for water, and *geiton*, neighbour, referring to the habitat of these plants). These very attractive aquatic perennials can be cultivated in fairly shallow or deep water. There are several species but *A. distachyos* is superior to all others. Also known as Cape pond weed or water hawthorn on account of the flowers' having a delicious hawthorn fragrance. It is one of the most desirable aquatics for garden ponds of all sizes, except the very smallest, and is adaptable also for lakes and in depths ranging from 1ft (30cm) to about 4ft (1.2m), where the leaves and flowers will be correspondingly larger. It has a tuberous rootstock that enlarges to the depth it is grown in although water from 18in (45cm) to 2ft (60cm) deep seems to be the optimum. The flowers, which are pure white with jet black anthers, are forked from a single spike. The leaves are oblong, lanceolate, bright green, sometimes blotched brown, on long stems, and float on the surface. It flowers freely during the spring, followed by a period of dormancy in the summer, and flowers again in the autumn. Occasionally it flowers during mild spells in mid-winter. They are easily grown, thriving in ordinary soil and are propagated by division of the tubers or by seed. The best time to divide is in the spring just before growth starts but more usually it is easier to grow them from seed.

In its native land, the Cape of Good Hope, the tubers of the *Aponogeton* were once cooked and eaten by the indigenous South African population.

Nuphar (Order Nymphaeaceae)

While *Nymphaea alba*, the white water lily, is regarded as the glory of the lake, then *Nuphar lutea*, the yellow water lily, is in its own unique way equally beautiful. The yellow globular flowers, which are curiously primeval, stand on strong stems just above the huge, almost circular, glossy green foliage that floats on the water surface. The strangely brandy-scented flowers are often 2in (5cm) across. They are found growing in fairly fast-flowing currents of British rivers and creeks but the massive rootstocks render them unsuitable for garden ponds.

Nuphar pumilum is suitable for such ponds. This is a dwarf form found growing in small lakes in Scotland. The small yellow flowers

Aponogeton distachyos *showing leaf, root and flower spike.*

Nuphar lutea.

are only an inch or so across when fully open. The unusually attractive translucent underwater foliage makes it an ideal plant for a pool or aquarium. Then there is a Japanese form, *Nuphar japonicum* 'Rubrotinctum', which is very similar to the preceding except that the flowers are orange-scarlet. *Nuphar advena* is a native of North America and is a vigorous species in which the leaves and flowers rise well above the surface of the water.

All the nuphars described are hardy and should be planted using the same method as for the water lilies.

Nymphoides (order Gentianaceae)

Nymphoides peltata (*Villarsia nymphoides*, *Limnanthemum nymphoides*) is also known as floating heart or water fringe. *Limnanthemum* comes from *Limne* a marsh or pool, and *anthemum*, a blossom. An aquatic flourishing in slow streams and ponds mainly in eastern England. The bright-yellow flowers some 1½in (4cm) across are prettily fringed. They are borne in clusters on the leaf stalks. The orbicular-shaped leaves float on the surface. A beautiful aquatic but difficult to eradicate once established on account of its rapidly growing runners.

2
PLANTING WATER LILIES

Water lilies are sun-loving plants so it would be reasonable to expect the siting of a garden pond to be in the sunniest part of the garden, or at least in a situation where the pool receives at least five hours of sun, preferably from midday onwards, when the day will be at its warmest. Under these conditions each individual bloom of a lily will last approximately five days. Falling leaves from overhanging trees can cause problems. Shelter from cold winds in the form of a wall, building or a hedge is an advantage. Most water lilies are rich feeders and make a lot of growth during a season, so ideally a heavy fibre-free loam should be used, but any good garden soil would be suitable. The addition of manure, peat or leaf-mould is not recommended since during its breakdown toxic gases are given off, causing discoloration of the water. Never use potting compost because this contains too much fertilizer of the wrong kind for the well-being of the lily. It also causes green water. Don't use mud from ponds or swamps as this is often sour and low in fertility and could contain troublesome aquatic weeds.

Planting lilies direct into the soil spread over the floor of the pool to a depth of 6–8in (15–20cm) and firming well is always preferable to using plastic baskets, as these restrict growth too much and require replanting in fresh soil every 3–4 years. It is like purchasing a shrub from a garden centre and then planting it without first removing the container. They will flower and flourish during the first season or so but will deteriorate thereafter through lack of essential plant nutrients. It is of course very important to select the most suitable varieties for the size of the pond, for there are lilies of varying degrees of vigour and spread to suit every size of pond or lake.

With the exception of the *pygmaea* varieties, water lilies require a minimum of 10–12in (25–30cm) of water covering the roots to an optimum depth of 20in (50cm) for most. At this depth you will probably find blanketweed less troublesome, simply because the water will be that much cooler, which tends to inhibit its growth, while the warmer water in shallow pools encourages its spread.

Therefore *pygmaea* varieties growing in small shallow pools or sinks may need more attention to keep the algae (blanketweed) at bay, but at least the pools will be of an easily manageable size.

In large ponds where spreading a 6in (15cm) layer of soil is totally impractical, construct rough enclosures with old bricks or weathered concrete blocks, not cemented together but with gaps to allow the roots the freedom of unrestricted growth. For lilies of moderate growth an enclosure of 2–3ft (60–90cm) in diameter would be sufficient, and for lilies of vigorous growth an enclosure of 3ft (1m) would be adequate. Fill with soil to a depth of between 6 and 8in (15 and 20cm) and firm well. If you have no alternative but to use containers, then use plastic laundry baskets. In a basket 2ft by 1ft 5in by 10in deep (60 × 42 × 25cm) the lily has room to expand and will not need to be divided or replanted for many years. Moving a basket of this size filled with soil into a pond can be a daunting proposition, but one way to overcome this would be to first place the basket into the empty pool and then fill it with soil. It may be necessary to line the basket with some sacking or hessian liners to prevent the soil running through the holes (a pool made from a Butyl pool liner is tough enough to walk on in rubber boots without damaging it) and then proceed with the method of planting as described. A stout plank or planks placed between the basket or brick container and the pool edge can be used to prevent possible damage, particularly if the subsoil is of a stony nature.

Water lilies are perennials by nature – their leaves die down in the autumn and the new growth emerges the following spring – but, unlike terrestrial perennials, they are transplanted when growth is active. Late April, May and June are the ideal months to plant in the Northern Hemisphere. At this time the water is warming up and the new leaves have started into growth but are not so far advanced as to cause any undue setback. There is no advantage in planting any earlier. Planting can, of course, be carried out during July and August. At this time, reduce the foliage and shorten the roots. The lilies will soon recover and make new growth, becoming established before the onset of the colder and shorter daylight hours of the autumn.

Before the actual planting is done there are two distinct groups of water lily rootstocks or rhizomes to consider. First, the rhizomes of the *tuberosa* and *odorata* forms are horizontally elongated underground roots which give rise to erect annual stems which bear foliage and flowers. The water lilies in this group should be planted horizontally just below the soil level but with the crown protruding above the soil.

Once established, the rhizomes branch out in various directions from the original centre and the plant often occupies a new position each year. This rhizome habit probably more than any other occupies more space because of its adventitious roots and erect stems and leaves which sprout at various points on the rhizome. The older parts gradually decay, so that the branches become isolated as separated plants.

A point worth bearing in mind is that the lilies in this group do not readily lend themselves to growing in aquatic containers – far better to plant them direct into the soil.

The second group, which really covers all the other varieties of water lilies, has rhizomes which grow vertically. In reality these rhizomes consist of short thick stems which elongate and enlarge each year. Planting lilies in this group could not be easier. Simply set the plant into the soil with its roots well spread out, and with the crown just exposed and firm well.

When planting direct into the soil on the floor of the pool it is must easier if water is allowed to run in slowly to a depth of between 2 and 3in (5–8cm). Leave for a few days to warm up and then plant. Increase the depth gradually as the growth of the leaves increases. This method reduces the check the plants would otherwise receive if the full depth of cold water was introduced at once.

If planting into baskets, use moist soil, firm well, and cover the top with a layer of shingle to prevent the soil from becoming dislodged. Sometimes it may be necessary to water the containers first before introducing them to the pool to prevent any air pockets. Lower the baskets carefully into the pool, applying the same principle of adding the water as advised for the other methods of planting.

Planting lilies into large or natural ponds which are difficult to empty sometimes requires a different method, particularly if the water is about 3ft (90cm) deep or so. Wrap the plant between two thick turves with the grass removed and secure with cord which will eventually rot. Drop these carefully into the pond, ensuring that the rhizome is facing the right way up and making sure that there is no chance of the lily becoming loose and subsequently floating to the surface.

Some consideration should be given to the choice of water that is to be introduced to a newly built pool. This is sometimes overlooked as possibly the first and only option is tap water, which is chemically treated to render it suitable for human consumption. However, this supply can have an adverse effect on ornamental fish if these are introduced almost straight away, and I am also convinced that tap water is conducive to green water and the formation of algae. It can therefore be very advantageous to construct ponds either in late summer or in the autumn and then allow the rain to fill them up naturally. Before planting time in the following spring, just siphon off the top 6in (15cm) or so of water and then plant in a natural chemical-free water. With a certain amount of luck the spring showers will fill and complete the pool.

Both well and spring water are very satisfactory but they are very cold in summer so they should be allowed to warm to the ambient temperature before the introduction of any water plants. Water lilies above all need to be in still and relatively warm water to flower satisfactory.

The two most satisfactory ways of purchasing water lilies are by mail order and from garden centres. There are still a few specialized nurseries which sell water lilies and aquatics by mail order. They have a much more extensive range than many garden centres can offer and it is worth writing for their catalogues. These plants are sent out from late April, May and June as washed bare-root plants, their roots and foliage trimmed, and packed in polythene bags, in which they travel satisfactorily by post.

Purchasing from garden centres enables you to select the plant you want. Choose the lilies that are established and growing in an open-weave plastic basket. Never be tempted to buy loose plants floating about in tanks of water with just a price tag attached to the rhizome. Their life in this condition is but a few days; they then begin to disintegrate.

Some garden centres stock lilies growing in 'solid' containers – containers without an adequate number of holes. Water lilies growing this way quickly become pot-bound and will often prove difficult to grow out of the cramped entanglement of thick white roots.

3
PROPAGATION

In the normal course of events, most keen gardeners like to try their skills at raising a few plants from material collected from their own garden, whether by taking cuttings from shrubs, perennials or alpines, or simply raising a variety of plants from seed. But when it comes to water lilies it is usually a matter of thinning out overgrown clumps, retaining just one suitable crown or rhizome for replanting and dumping what is not required.

So often the lilies that have occupied these old-established ponds turn out to be either N. × marliacea 'Carnea', a once most popular pink but too vigorous for most garden pools, or N. × marliacea 'Albida', equally popular and vigorous. Another well-known variety is 'Gladstoniana', a fine large white – totally unsuitable for garden ponds but unsurpassed for lakes. These three varieties are so widespread in ponds both large and small that there is virtually no demand for the surplus crowns when the time comes for them to be thinned out.

However, if by some chance you have a large pond or lake full of N. 'Escarboucle' or N. 'James Brydon' in need of a good thinning out, you will find far fewer surplus planting crowns from these varieties than from N. × marliacea 'Carnea' or 'Gladstoniana' of similar age and in similar conditions. This is because both 'Escarboucle' and 'James Brydon' are very shy in producing propagating material, and the prices in nurserymen's catalogues reflect this. While N. 'Escarboucle' does not spread in the same way as N. × marliacea 'Carnea', it is nevertheless a lily of a strong constitution. From a nurseryman's point of view, therefore, it is important to encourage propagating material from these shy producers by growing them in shallow water to hasten the production of 'eyes'.

Since these are all hybrids they cannot be raised from seed. Propagation from hybrids can be achieved only through vegetative reproduction since hybrids are generally sterile. The essential element in reproduction is the system of a cell, or group of cells, which if detached from the parent plant possesses the capacity of independent development and so can be called the offspring.

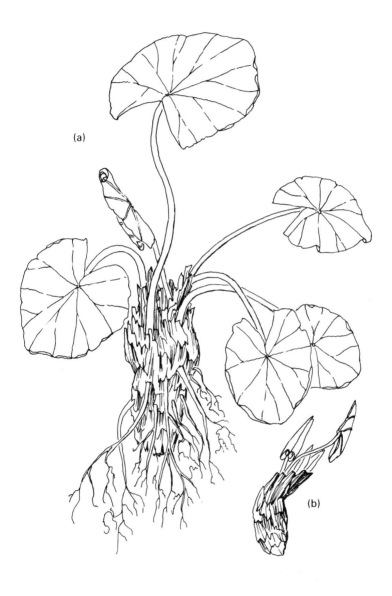

(a)

(b)

A vertically grown rhizome of Nymphaea *showing habit (a) and detached eye for propagation (b).*

Raising hardy water lilies from seed is confined to the species, including *N. pygmaea* and the *odorata* forms.

So vegetative propagation is the most widely used method of reproduction of water lilies and it requires no great skill on the part of the keen gardener to raise a few plants, particularly some of the scarce hybrids or those varieties which are shy in propagating material. The variety *N.* × *marliacea* 'Chromatella' is prone to producing an abundance of propagating material.

Lift an established plant during the growing season (May or June are the ideal months), wash off the mud and, using a sharp knife, trim back the roots and foliage. On the rhizome a number of 'eyes' or offsets will be seen. These appear as buds. With the aid of a sharp knife carefully remove the 'eyes', plant them in a bowl (a washing-up bowl is ideal) containing about 3in (7.5cm) of sterilized sifted loam, then cover with 2in (5cm) of water. The parent plant can now be replanted in the pool. Between ten and twelve eyes can be accommodated in a bowl and they will begin rooting within a few weeks. Stand the bowl outside in a sunny situation during the summer but remove it to a cold frame or greenhouse during the winter months. The following spring the 'eyes' will have made enough growth to both roots and foliage to be transplanted safely to permanent positions in garden pools. Transplant them first in shallow water and gradually increase the depth as the lily becomes established and the leaves lengthen. It will be another year or so before the plants reach flowering size.

Many aquatic plants can be successfully propagated vegetatively. With some it is a matter of dividing the rootstocks in much the same way as for herbaceous plants except that ideally aquatics are lifted from the ponds during the growing season in April and May, though I find that *Caltha* species are best divided during September. Lifting and replanting the plants at this time ensures that the plants are well established for flowering during the following spring. *Caltha palustris* and *C. palustris alba* can also be grown from seed sown directly after gathering.

Iris laevigata varieties soon become congested grown either in aquatic baskets or in pockets of a garden pool and require dividing from time to time. This is best done directly after flowering. Split the clumps up into single plants, trim the roots and shorten the foliage to prevent excessive transpiration. Replant in fresh soil.

Plants such as *Myosotis palustris*, *Veronica beccabunga* and *Mentha aquatica* are easily divided during April by carefully pulling the matted clumps apart and retaining the young outer pieces for planting back in fresh soil and shallow water. The central portion

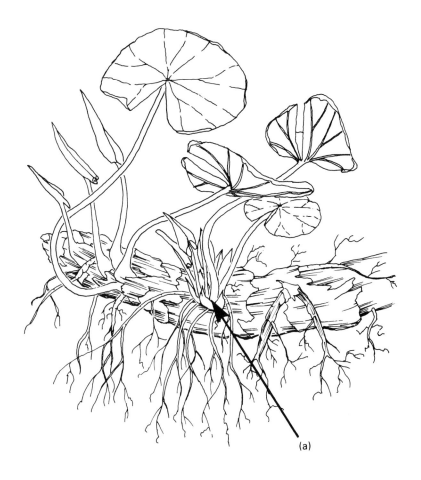

A horizontal rhizome of an odorata *form of* Nymphaea *showing habit and a propagating eye (a).*

of the clump is best discarded. Late April or early May is the best time for dividing *Scirpus tabernaemontani* 'Albescens' and *S. t.* 'Lacustris'. *S. t.* 'Zebrinus' needs dividing and replanting in fresh soil every 2–3 years in order to maintain the attractive zebra stripes in the stems, otherwise they will become a uniform shade of green. Clumps of *Pontederia* can be lifted and divided into separate plants with the aid of a sharp knife in early May. Replant in fresh soil.

Of the water lilies that can be grown from seed, the most important is *Nymphaea pygmaea alba*. This species does not produce any 'eyes' or offsets so the only means of propagation is by seed. All the *odorata* forms set fertile seed pods but they can also be propagated vegetatively like the hybrids.

(a)

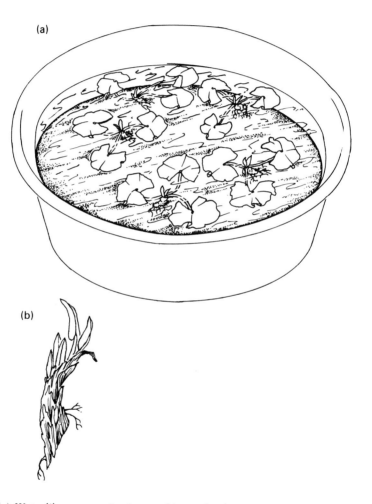

(b)

(a) Water lily eyes growing in a washing-up bowl containing 3in (7.5cm) of sifted loam and approximately 2in (5cm) of water. Eyes taken during May or June will be well established for planting in the pond the following spring. But for the first few weeks, cover with just 6in (15cm) of water. (b) Eye ready for planting.

Developing seeds are protected from transpiration and from other dangers by the ovary wall, which thickens and hardens into the fruit wall or pericarp. Seeds as a class are the most xerophytic of plant structures and even hydrophytes are generally covered with hard and impermeable coats.

During late August and September the ripened pods of *N. pygmaea alba* will burst and the seeds will first float on the surface of the water for a few hours before sinking to the bottom of the pool, so you will need to be fairly vigilant and collect the seeds before they sink. Sow them right away (as dried seed rarely germinates) in a bowl containing about 3in (7.5cm) of sifted sterilized loam and cover with about 1in (2.5cm) of water. Keep the bowl in a frost-free greenhouse or conservatory until the following spring, when germination will take place. Keep the water free from any algae that might form as this could hinder the growth of the young seedlings. When the seedlings are large enough to handle they can be carefully transplanted into more bowls or potted up individually into 3in (7.5cm) pots using similar sifted loam that is free from fertilizer, peat and sand. Cover with 2in (5cm) of water. Plant out into their permanent positions in July. Flowering normally takes place within a year of the seed being sown.

Other aquatic plants that can be grown successfully from seed are *Pontederia*, *Aponogeton distachyos*, *Orontium* and *Lysichiton* species. In all instances the seed should be sown as soon as it is ripe in bowls of loam using the same procedure as for *N. pygmaea alba*, though you may find it easier to sow the *Orontium* seeds individually into 3in (7.5cm) pots and place the pots into bowls of water. These will be ready for planting out during the following spring or summer. The *Pontederia* seed will not germinate until the following spring. *Iris kaempferi* and *I. laevigata* may be sown during the spring in seed trays using standard sowing compost and placed in a cold frame or greenhouse and kept watered in the normal way without the need for submerging the trays in water. Prick out the seedlings when large enough to handle into 3in (7cm) pots using a standard potting compost. They should be ready for planting out in their final positions during late summer.

4
SUBMERGED AQUATIC PLANTS AND FLOATING PLANTS

SUBMERGED AQUATICS

These aquatic plants are also known as oxygenating plants or, using the vernacular, pondweeds. In many instances this is exactly what they are, often choking out the more desirable occupants of a pond within a few weeks of their introduction. Chosen with care, certain varieties of these submerged aquatics are essential to the well-being of a pond. Under the influence of light they liberate oxygen and absorb carbon dioxide. This is of great importance to ornamental fish, which do the opposite by breathing oxygen and giving off carbon dioxide.

The plants also play an important part in maintaining clear water by creating a certain amount of shade from strong sunlight.

The foliage and the congested stems of the plants make an ideal spawning area in which the fish can breed and also a place where the young fry can seek refuge from their cannabilistic parents once they have hatched.

Many of the plants are extremely attractive, particularly their underwater foliage, which in some plants differs from the surface leaves. Most are easily grown from cuttings rooted into soil during May or June. After July the stems become too brittle to transplant successfully.

The usual method of planting is by attaching unrooted bunches to a small piece of lead and dropping them into the pool. This method, however, is satisfactory only if the bunch happens to land on a bed of soil. It is far better to plant a bunch or two in a planting basket of soil, covering the top with a layer of shingle in order to prevent disturbance by fish. Place the baskets on the bottom of the pool, where the stems will soon lengthen and grow up to the surface.

Plants

Callitriche

Several species are found growing in small, cool streams and ponds throughout the British Isles. Whilst it is often called water starwort because of its surface appearance, the underwater leaves are thinner and appear quite different. The tangled foliage is usually swarming with various aquatic insects and crustacea. Although many of these are natural fish foods, it is advisable to rinse this and all other plants before planting them into garden ponds.

C. autumnalis This is one of the few that are active during the winter months. Always entirely submerged with tiny dark-green foliage. This is the best oxygenator of the family.
C. verna This is the commonest form, with its surface foliage forming thick bright-green rosettes. Not one of the best oxygenating plants but makes a good haven and natural food for fish.

Ceratophyllum

C. demersum (hornwort) Found growing in Britain and Europe, this plant has dense narrow dark-green brittle foliage, resembling miniature bottle-brush plants. It is an excellent oxygenator and requires just 'dropping' into the pond: although not a floating plant, it does have roots which in time find their way to the soil base. It is also capable of growing in great depths. This plant is easily thinned out if the need arises. In the winter months the plant sinks to the bottom of the pond in the form of buds until growth begins in the spring. A first choice for all ponds.

Chara (Stonewort)

The members of this family are found growing in still waters in Britain. Most have rough, bristly stems and leaves on branching growths. It spreads quickly and has an unpleasant smell when handled. During the summer the stems and foliage develop calcareous deposits which become encrusted and remain preserved after the plant has died down and decayed.

C. aspera This plant has very slender stems with branching foliage of pale greenish white.
C. vulgaris The greenish-grey branching stems are a foot or so long. Other species include *C. fragilis* and *C. hispida*.

Eleocharis

E. acicularis (hairgrass)   Hairgrass grows to a dense tufted mass of green spiky grass no more than 1in (2.5cm) high. It spreads rapidly on the base of the pool, giving the appearance of an underwater lawn.

Elodea

Known to the Americans as anacharis and in Europe as *Elodea*, it is also popularly called Canadian pondweed. *Elodea* is a first-class oxygenating plant but unfortunately it can become too vigorous for the larger pond or lake, where it can be difficult to control. However, it is more easily controlled in moderate-sized ponds. Not the first choice of oxygenators.

E. crispa   A very distinct form with large dark-green reflexed leaves on long stems. An excellent oxygenator and suitable for all but the smallest pools. Some gardeners curse it as an uncontrollable weed.

Fontinalis

F. antipyretica (willow moss)   A native plant that has evergreen long branching dark feathery moss-like foliage adaptable to sun or shady conditions. These plants are often found attached to stones in slow-moving streams. Legend has it that the dried foliage was once used by Scandinavians to pack between the walls and chimneys of their wooden houses to exclude air and to reduce the risk of fire. An excellent oxygenator and a most suitable spawning ground for fish.

Hottonia

H. palustris (water violet)   One of the few oxygenating plants with very beautiful flowers. Stout stems that rise 6–12in (15–30cm) out of the water with whorls of small white to pale lavender flowers in early summer with the underwater foliage of a delicate green and finely dissected. In the autumn *Hottonia* forms winter buds which sink in the mud and growth restarts in the spring. Not the easiest of plants to establish.

Myriophyllum

M. verticillatum (whorled water milfoil)   Delicate very finely cut leaves arranged in whorls round branching stems. An attractive oxygenating plant for the small pool.

M. spicatum (spiked water milfoil)   Very similar in appearance to the above species except that *M. spicatum* has long flower spikes with red petals just showing above the water level.

Potamogeton

P. crispus (curled pondweed)   The attractive curly foliage is almost translucent and of a dark green to reddish bronze in colour.

P. densus (opposite-leaved pondweed)   A distinct form with slender hair on fennel-like foliage.

Ranunculus

R. aquatilis (water crowfoot)   A common plant found in ponds and streams but not to be confused with *R. fluitans*, river crowfoot, which is often seen in great masses on rivers. *R. aquatilis* has wedge-shaped floating leaf segments with branched stems carrying white buttercup-like flowers held above the water in spring and dying down late in the summer. The submerged foliage is finely cut into hair-like segments. A good oxygenator and worth growing for the flowers alone.

Tilloea

T. recurva   A succulent aquatic introduced to Britain in 1927 from Australia. Bright-green fleshy leaves carrying tiny white star-like flowers during the summer. Of vigorous growth, its ease of self-propagation makes it one of the most pernicious aquatics ever introduced, which condemns it as an oxygenating plant. Thoroughly undesirable and not to be recommended in any water garden.

OXYGENATING PLANTS AT A GLANCE

Oxygenating plants are essential for the well-being of a garden pond but the question is, what are the best varieties to introduce and how many?

My experience has proved conclusively that no particular formula of planting so many oxygenating plants for each square foot or metre of water can be applied. If only one or two bunches of certain kinds are planted during May (the best month for planting) in a pond of average size (10 × 7ft; 3 × 2m) and both bunches grow then it is almost certain that you will be thinning them out by the barrowful a few months later – enough to supply the neighbourhood. You need to be even more cautious if you are considering any kind of planting in larger natural ponds or lakes, simply because once established it will be virtually impossible to keep growth under control. Therefore the choice is important. I have listed a selection of six plants which are attractive and which are either easy to control or do not spread so rapidly as others.

Best Oxygenating Plants for Garden Ponds

Callitriche autumnalis   Active during the winter, dark-green underwater foliage.

Ceratophyllum demersum (hornwort)   Perhaps the most universally accepted plant that is most suited for garden ponds and lakes.

Hottonia palustris (water violet)   The delicate underwater foliage and the attractive violet flowers in the spring make this one of the most beautiful of oxygenating plants, but often difficult to establish. It is best planted in spring (April); unlike most other oxygenators, *Hottonia* rarely grows successfully as unrooted bunches after April.

Myriophyllum venticillatum   Attractive foliage – an acceptable plant for the small pond.

Potamogeton crispus   I have never seen this plant become an uncontrollable mass. The underwater foliage makes this a desirable plant.

Ranunculus aquatilis (water crowfoot)   The white buttercup-like flowers make this an attractive feature during April. The submerged leaves are very finely cut into hair-like segments. Not likely to become a nuisance in any pond or lake.

The following five oxygenating plants are not recommended in garden ponds or lakes:

Eleocharis acicularis (hairgrass)   This is better suited to an indoor aquarium than any garden pond.

Elodea canadensis   Although a good oxygenator, its rapid growth makes this plant unsuitable for all ponds and lakes.

Elodea crispa   Certainly more attractive than the previous one, but this is also very vigorous once established.
Chara (stonewort)   A rapidly spreading plant which makes it unsuitable for garden ponds.
Tilloea recurva   A tough and uncompromising plant that should never be introduced into any pond or lake.

FLOATING AQUATICS

Many of these floating aquatics are among the most interesting and beneficial plants in a garden pond and used in conjunction with submerged aquatics they help create the correct balance of plant life and maintain clear water. During the summer they flourish and obtain the nutrients they require from the water, though some of the plants do send down roots which reach the bottom of the pool.

Floating aquatics provide shade to the surface of the water. This greatly reduces the chance of blanketweed forming an unsightly nuisance. The fibrous roots provide a haven in which fish can breed and young fry shelter from any predators.

During the winter most sink to the bottom of the pond, either in the form of terminal buds or dormant seeds, only to surface again as young plants the following spring.

It is inevitable that some overcrowding will occur among certain plants and so thinning out becomes necessary. This is best done in the spring or autumn.

Plants

Azolla

A. caroliniana (fairy floating moss)   Pale-green fronds turning to red in the summer. Forms dense mats that spread rapidly but is easily killed by frosts. If left unchecked it will spread so rapidly that it will exclude all light from the pond, to the extent that young water lilies can suffer and possibly die.

Eichhornia

E. crassipes (floating water hyacinth)   One of the most attractive of all floating aquatics. The shiny rounded leaves have swollen stems that act as buoyancy floats and the thick feathery black roots are invaluable for fish breeding since they make an ideal haven for spawning. The particularly beautiful lavender flowers are produced in late summer outside, but often fail to bloom in a dull wet summer. This is a tropical plant which in an outside pool survives only during the frost-free months. However, it does make an ideal subject for any indoor pool or aquarium. *Eichhornia* spreads rapidly in the warm waters of the tropics, so much so that it chokes navigational waterways in its native countries in the Middle East and Africa. Propagation is by cutting through the rooted runners. Plants that have spent the summer months in an outside pool must be removed into frost-free quarters for the winter. Keep a few packed close together in a bowl of soil and water until the following spring or after the danger of frost has gone. It is often easier to treat them as annuals and to obtain new plants each season.

Hydrocharis

H. morsus-ranae (frog-bit)   A native plant to Britain with bright-green circular leaves little more than 1in (2.5cm) in diameter with tiny three-petalled pure-white flowers. The plants spread slowly by runners. During the autumn the plants are reduced to winter buds, which sink to the bottom of the pool. They surface as young plants in late May or early June. An ideal floating aquatic for the smallest pool or tub.

Lemna (Duckweed)

The genus comprises native British species found floating on stagnant ponds. They cover the water with small floating leaves with most having a root to each frond or leaf. Most spread so rapidly that they are recommended only for introduction to the smallest pond or tub where they can be easily controlled. However, the duckweeds are of value as food for goldfish and for maintaining clear water. It is important to have at least one-third of the water free from *lemna*.

L. gibba (Gibbon's duckweed)   A rare species which has hemi-spherical fronds ½–⅓in (about 1cm) in diameter. A useful food for fish.
L. minor (lesser duckweed)   The commonest form with ovate light-green fronds budding freely. A single root from each frond grows down into the water.
L. polyrrhiza (great duckweed)   A rare native with the individual

fronds ¼–½in (about 1cm) in diameter, each frond having many roots. This is the largest of all duckweeds.

L. *trisulca* (ivy-leaved duckweed) The most useful of the four species, being much less invasive than any of the preceding. A pretty plant that floats just below the water surface. *Lemna trisulca* has translucent fronds which grow at right angles to each other. An excellent plant for maintaining clear water.

Stratiotes

S. *aloides* (water soldier) A curious plant native to the United Kingdom found in ponds and ditches often in abundance locally. The narrow sword-shaped serrated leaves are arranged in the form of a shuttlecock. The plant remains submerged for a considerable period, surfacing from May to July to produce a three-petalled flower in the axil of the leaves. Once the flowers have faded the plant submerges and remains at the bottom of the pool. In spring each parent plant gives rise to a number of runners or offspring. These are best removed from the parent, which is then discarded, and the young offspring returned to the pool, where they will soon send down roots reaching to the base of the pool to act as an anchor and to maintain stability. A useful plant for all but the smallest pool, provided that they are kept under control.

Trapa

The name is shortened from *calcitrapa*, from *caltrops*, the Latin name of an instrument furnished with four iron spikes and formerly used in war to impede the progress of cavalry. Water caltrops are a small genus of curious tropical and hardy floating plants from central and southern Europe through to Asia and Africa. Small white flowers give rise to large bony fruits with four angles or spines which do not open and have a short circular beak at the top.

T. *natans* (Jesuit's nut, water chestnut) A rare species from southern Europe. The seeds or fruits are large (up to ¾–1in; 2.5cm broad) and four-angled, all with sharp spines. These fruits give rise to floating rosettes of triangular or rhomboidal leaves of a rich olive green or ruby red. The plants are kept afloat by swollen petioles.

Cultivation could not be easier. It is a matter of throwing the fruits into the water in the spring. Treat them as annuals, as the fruits do not ripen sufficiently in temperate climates.

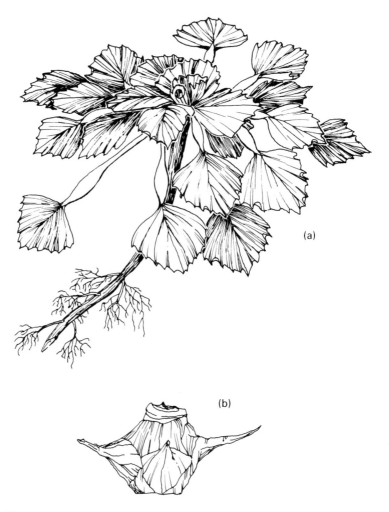

(a)

(b)

Trapa natans *showing rosettes of floating leaves* (a) and *fruit of* Trapa natans (b).

Utricularia

The name is derived from *utriculus*, a small bag or cavity, alluding to the minute pitcher-like bodies or bladders developed on the leaves and stems. The bladderworts, as they are more commonly known, are represented by a number of species native to the British Isles. They are hardy carnivorous aquatic plants whose vegetative parts float just below the water surface and only the flowering stem of some 6–8in (15–20cm) protrude out of the water. The mass of slender stems and leaves bear a profusion of minute pitchers or bladders. These are visible to the naked eye. Each bladder entraps microscopic aquatic animal life. The entrapped animalcules are not poisoned, however, but as they cannot escape they eventually die in the trap and their bodies provide food for the bladderwort.

U. intermedia, U. minor, U. neglecta and *U. vulgaris*   These are all similar bladderworts. The first two have pale-yellow snapdragon-like flowers protruding several inches out of the water and the latter two have rich yellow flowers. All species flower from July to August. After the flowers fade and die the plants form compact winter buds and fall to the bottom of the water, where they remain until the following spring when they start growing actively again.

5
MARGINAL AQUATIC PLANTS

The aquatics listed in this chapter are all perfectly hardy in the British Isles and perennial unless otherwise stated. Most require their rootstocks submerged in water of varying depths, although I find that some species and varieties are better suited growing in mud or with at most an inch of water covering the roots. The reason is that deeper water impairs their flowering potential.

The marginal plants are not considered essential for the well-being of a pool but they do contribute colour and diversity of shape and form from March through until early September. They also consume certain nutrients from the water and soil which could otherwise cause green water and the formation of algae.

The marginal plants are adaptable for growing in pockets of small ponds or the margins and edges of larger ponds and streams, but care must be taken when making a choice. The creeping stoloniferous rootstocks of some types of these plants can penetrate the soft mud with ease and become a nuisance.

I have never advocated the use of plastic planting containers for aquatic plants, whatever the size or type of pond. In fibreglass or prefabricated pools the tops of the containers often show and are difficult to camouflage. Often there is no alternative to using aquatic baskets. However, if space allows, instead of containers, try using some suitable natural rock to form a pocket, then fill this with soil to an approximate depth of 5in (12.5cm) and plant one variety in each pocket. You will find the results far more natural and attractive, particularly when the pool itself is an artificial creation.

Controlling rampant plants in a small pond can be relatively easy but nevertheless an unnecessary time-consuming operation. The larger natural ponds pose a much more serious problem. Placing sheets of slate vertically in the pool to form a pocket in which to restrict the plants is one method. Ideally, such rampant subjects should not be introduced initially. The plants are clearly identified in the following list.

For planting, use the same good garden soil that is free from manures and peat as recommended for the water lilies.

PLANTS

Acorus (Order Araceae) (Sweet Flag)

A. calamus The sword-shaped wavy-edged foliage of this plant is aromatic when crushed. The tough rhizomatous roots have the same fragrance. A suitable plant for growing on the edges of larger ponds and on the banks of a stream. Propagation is by dividing the roots in the spring.

Introduced to Great Britain from eastern Europe and Asia in about the sixteenth century. It is now naturalized mainly in East Anglia, England.

A. calamus 'Variegatus This is a very attractive form of the preceding plain-green species. The pink and cream shoots in the early spring give rise to cream-and-green sword-shaped foliage which is in character right through the summer months. It has the same fragrant foliage as the preceding species and, growing to about 2½–3ft (75–90cm) is a most desirable plant for the garden pond as it is not so vigorous. Best grown in 1–3in (2.5–7.5cm) of water.

A. gramineus A dwarf Japanese species suitable for growing in either a very wet position or shallow water. Tufts of thick dark foliage only about 6in (15cm) high.

A. gramineus 'Variegatus' A variegated form of the preceding, with dark-green narrow foliage edged creamy yellow, ideally suited for small shallow pools and sink gardens. It grows to 6in (15cm). Best grown in just wet soil or an inch of water. Propagation is by division of the clumps in the spring.

Alisma (Order Alismataceae) (Water Plantain)

A genus composed entirely of hardy aquatic species. They are most easily grown, thriving in shallow water in ponds and the margins of lakes and streams. Remove the old flower heads regularly to prevent the many seeds that readily germinate from becoming a nuisance.

A. parviflora (American water plantain) A comparatively rare North American species that has whorls of tiny three-petalled rose-

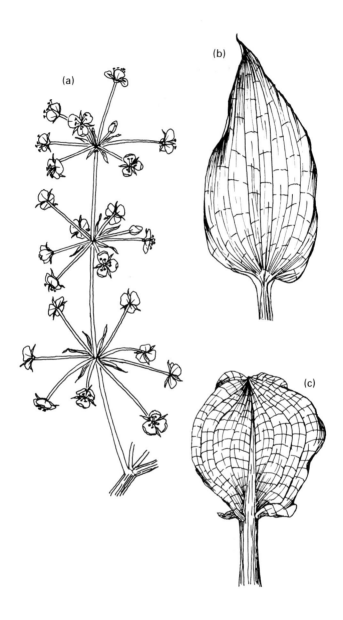

A portion of the flower head of Alisma plantago-aquatica (a),
a leaf of Alisma plantago-aquatica (b) and *a leaf of* Alisma
parviflora (c).

white flowers on 18in (45cm) stems. The dark-green foliage is conspicuously rounded and ribbed.

A. plantago-aquatica (water plantain) A free-flowering British native thriving in shallow water beside ponds and streams. The broad ovate leaves are ribbed and the 3ft (90cm) pyramidal stems are clothed with whorls of tiny three-petalled rose-white flowers. A handsome aquatic for naturalizing by lakes.

A. lanceolatum (lanceolate water plantain) Very similar in appearance to the preceding species except that it is less tall at 1½ft (45cm).

Butomus (Order Butomaceae)

The name comes from *bous*, an ox, and *temno*, to cut, referring to the sharp leaves which injure the mouths of cattle feeding on them.

B. umbellatus (flowering rush, water gladiolus) One of the most beautiful of our native aquatics, found growing near ponds and ditches on marshy ground. It has triangular sedge-like radical leaves, rising from a thick rootstock, which are tinged purple when young, eventually turning green. Smooth round stems some 3ft (90cm) tall bear umbels of rose-pink flowers. The slowly spreading clumps will need dividing and replanting every two years to ensure that the plant continues flowering. Well worth growing in ponds and lakes alike.

Calla (Order Araceae) (Bog Arum)

C. palustris The spreading rhizome-like stems grow at the water's edge in 2–3in (5–7cm) of water or sometimes spread further into the pool, anchoring themselves in the mud with long white roots. The species has heart-shaped shiny green foliage with pure-white arum-like flowers. The flowers are normally pollinated by pond snails clambering over them and by late summer the female flowers will form clusters of bright-red berries. Growing to a height of about 6in (15cm), it is a useful plant for masking the hard edges of fibreglass ponds.

Caltha (Order Ranunculaceae)

A genus of early-flowering plants for very wet soil or shallow water no deeper than an inch in full sun or partial shade, where they will flower regularly year after year. Propagation is either by seed

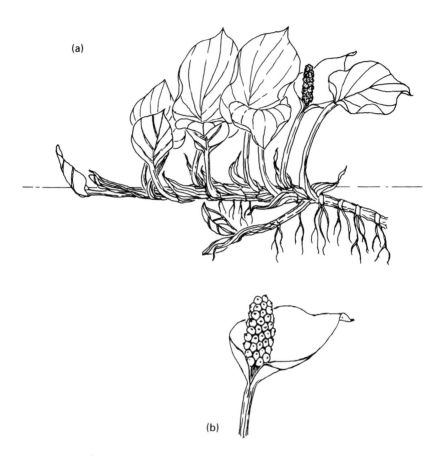

(a)

(b)

Calla palustris *showing flowering plant (a) and detached female flower with berries (b)*.

sown directly after gathering or by division of the clumps in September.

C. leptosepala From North America, this species is comparatively rare and more slow-growing than the others. Not a spectacular plant, but it has single silvery-white flowers on 6in (15cm) stems with small rounded dark-green leaves. It can be grouped amongst other slow-growing marsh plants.

C. palustris   Marsh marigold, kingcup and Mary-blob are alternative names for one of the most beautiful native plants found growing in damp meadows and marshes throughout Britain. The bright-yellow flowers are borne in great profusion on branched stems some 12–18in (30–45cm) high amongst the almost round dentate foliage. Well worth growing in any garden pond or a permanently damp area as it heralds the spring.

C. palustris alba   A native plant from the Himalayas. The creamy white buds begin to show through the mud as early as February, often before the foliage, forming a compact clump of single white flowers with greenish-yellow centres 6–9in (15–22cm) high. The dentated heart-shaped foliage is an attractive shade of green. Grows best in wet mud or damp soil.

C. palustris 'Plena' ('Multiplex')   A very showy plant flowering about a fortnight later than *Caltha palustris*. Its fully double true golden-yellow flowers practically cover the entire plant, giving the effect of foot-high mounds of gold, particularly effective near water. Very reliable and of easy culture for all ponds and waterside planting. Divide large clumps in September as it does not set seed.

C. palustris minor (*C. radicans*)   Found growing in the north of England and Scotland, an attractive plant, not often seen in gardens, flowering in May and June when the others have finished. The single yellow flowers are smaller and grow only to 1ft (30cm). It has a stoloniferous habit.

C. polypetala (giant marsh marigold)   The largest of all the species and the earliest to show its foliage, often in January. It does not produce a riot of colour, but the large buttercup-like flowers are on 2ft-long (60cm) stalks among the huge shiny foliage. Grown on the banks of the larger water garden, it will, by its vigorous stoloniferous habit, travel into the water, rooting into the mud as it goes. Not clump-forming and an unsuitable plant for the small pool, but ideal for large wet areas and lakeside plantings. Often in full flower by March.

C. tyermanii   Quite rare as it is not often seen in gardens. It has single yellow flowers on purplish trailing stems. Later-flowering than most others (May and June).

Cotula (order Compositae) (Golden Buttons)

C. coronopifolia   Raised annually from seed, this is a delightful plant bearing tiny yellow flowers on stems only a few inches high throughout the summer. Ideal for in an inch or so of water in small pools.

Eriophorum (Order Cyperaceae) (Cotton Grass)

Perennials which can be grown successfully in marshy ground or in a few inches of water – but really too vigorous for most garden pools.

E. augustifolium and *E. latifolium* are similar species growing 12–15in (30–42cm) high, with thin grassy foliage with fluffy cotton-wool-like inflorescences.

Houttuynia (Order Saururaceae)

H. cordata   A quick-spreading species that has bluish-green heart-shaped leaves tinged bronze-brown. The white four-petalled flowers are cone-shaped on foot-high reddish stems. It thrives in mud or shallow water. There is a double-flowered form, and both are reputed to have leaves scented like orange peel. Although it spreads rapidly in wet mud, severe winters will check much of its creeping root system but rarely will it be killed outright.

Hypericum (Order Guttiferae) (Marsh Hypericum, Marsh St John's Wort)

H. elodes   This attractive species has soft tomentose rounded leaves on creeping stems. A few clusters of soft yellow flowers appear in July and August. Requiring only an inch or so of water, it is a useful plant for growing on the margins of concrete or fibreglass pools, thus disguising the unsightly edges.

Iris (Order Iridaceae)

I. laevigata   From the Latin *laevis*, meaning smooth. This Japanese iris is closely related to *Iris kaempferi*. A very desirable group of aquatic plants for growing on the edges of ponds and margins of streams. They will grow in water up to 2in (5cm) deep, though I prefer to grow them in very wet mud. Water any deeper impairs their flowering ability. In June the first of two buds from each stem opens to clear three-petalled sky-blue flowers with a distinctive gold line running down the centre of each fall. The second bud opens as the first fades. Ample soft-green foliage. These irises can be grown from seed; there may be some variation of colour, but all should be good. To propagate plants that will be true to their parent, dividing the clumps into individual plants directly after flowering is the only method. *I. laevigata* 'Alba' is pure white and is a good contrast with *I. laevigata*, while 'Snowdrift' is the superlative form with six large white petals. 'Albo-purpurea' has blue flowers flecked with white. 'Colchesteri' and 'Monstrosa' are almost identical if not synonymous with each other. The six-petalled white flowers have deep-blue markings at the end of the falls. 'Muragamo' is similar to *I. laevigata* except that the flowers have six petals instead of three. *I. l. 'Variegata'* is a most beautiful form with sky-blue flowers. The striking green-and-white fan-shaped foliage is in character all summer. 'Rose Queen' is a hybrid between *I. laevigata* and *I. kaempferi*; it will grow satisfactorily in damp soil. With grass-like foliage, it is a little taller than *I. laevigata* and has dainty soft rose-pink flowers. All *I. laevigata* varieties grow to about 2ft (60cm).

I. pseudacorus (yellow flag, yellow water iris) The native British species found growing in wet fields, marshes and banks of streams. The sword-shaped leaves are some 3–4ft (90–120cm) long. The strong stems with bright-yellow flowers are followed by plenty of good seed heads. Too vigorous for growing in garden ponds. Useful, though, for colonizing at the edge of lakes and marshy ground. However, there are a number of interesting forms which are less vigorous: 'Bastardii' has lovely sulphur-yellow flowers and 'Golden Queen' has larger yellow flowers without the distinctive brown markings in the throat and falls.

I. pseudacorus 'Variegata' This variety of the yellow flag iris has spectacular spring foliage of cream edged with green. Less vigorous than the type, it is suitable for most garden ponds. From midsummer onwards the 3ft (90cm) leaves assume a uniform shade of green.

Juncus (Order Juncaceae)

A genus of over a hundred species of hardy annual and perennial rushes, usually with a rigid habit. The flowers are either green or brownish. In small umbels or panicles. Very few species are worth cultivating in the water garden, but *J. effusus* var. *spiralis*, the corkscrew rush, has a curious and contorted leaf form – a desirable plant for the flower arranger. It is not invasive and will grow satisfactorily at the water's edge of a garden pond. 2ft (60cm).

Mentha (Order Labiatae)

M. aquatica (water mint)   A common native found growing near ponds and ditches throughout the British Isles. It has strong purplish aromatic foliage with whorls of lavender flowers. I would be a little hesitant before introducing it to a pond or a bog garden on account of its vigorous spreading habit.

Menyanthes (Order Gentianaceae)

M. trifoliata (bog bean)   A most attractive native British species flourishing in very watery bogs or in water up to 9in (22cm) deep. The star-like flowers are white or blush inside and reddish outside, from purplish buds. Flowering in May and June, the petals are prettily fringed, giving the appearance of enlarged snowflakes. The rootstock is long and creeping, giving rise to trifoliate leaves similar to that of a broad bean. Easily propagated by division of the root.

Mimulus (Order Scrophulariaceae) (Monkey Flower)

The name comes from *mimo*, an ape, referring to the ringent corolla. A genus comprising over 70 species of hardy and half-hardy herbaceous perennial plants. They are well represented in northern and eastern America but the genus is totally absent from Europe and the whole of the Mediterranean region. All the herbaceous species and their varieties thrive best in very watery areas by the margins of streams and pools and in damp borders. The common musk, *M. moschatus*, is well known and is now naturalized in various parts of Britain. A form of this species had a notable musky fragrance throughout the plant but since about the turn of the century it appears to have been lost.

M. cardinalis   Erect growing perennials with large red flowers borne on branched stems from June to August. Light-green pubescent foliage. Sometimes the plants take on an untidy appearance during late summer. Trim them lightly to encourage new growth. Hardy in all but the coldest parts of Britain. Then a light covering of straw should be sufficient protection. Propagation is by division of the crowns in spring. 1–2ft (30–60cm).
M. cupreus   Coppery or crimson-coloured flowers over 6–9in (15–22cm) mounds of soft green foliage. This Chilean species, together with *M. guttatus*, has given rise to a number of showy

hybrids, including 'Bees' Dazzler' (crimson), 'Brilliant' (deep purple crimson), 'Red Emperor' (crimson scarlet), 'Whitecroft Scarlet' (vermilion), and others. Most come true from seed and sometimes plants do die out so raising plants from seed each spring is an easy and reliable method of propagation.

M. guttatus Very similar to *M. luteus*. Speckled.

M. luteus (common monkey flower) The yellow flower of this species has two dark red marks in the mouth of the corolla. The coarsely toothed leaves are glabrous on stems 9–12in (22–30cm) high and perennial in habit with densely matted stolons. There is a 'hose-in-hose' form. This is curiously double with one flower sitting inside the other.

M. moschatus (musk) This is a spreading perennial which liberates an abundance of seed that germinates easily in damp soil. Although pretty enough in a wild area it will soon become a nuisance in damp borders of a well-kept garden. The clumps have a clammy or woolly appearance and the small pale-yellow flowers are lightly spotted and splashed with brown. June to August. 2ft (60cm).

M. ringens A true aquatic from north-eastern America, flourishing in shallow water or mud. The 3ft (90cm) branching square stems of upright growth have narrow dark-green foliage. The lavender snapdragon-like flowers are smaller than the other members of the *Mimulus* genus and are in character from June to August. Hardy and perennial, it is an ideal plant for garden ponds of all sizes. Propagation is by cuttings taken during June and July rooted into mud and overwintered in a frame ready to plant out the following spring. Also by division of the roots in spring.

Myosotis (Order Boraginaceae) (Water Forget-Me-Not)

The name, used by Dioscorides, is derived from *muos*, a mouse, and *otos*, an ear, because of the appearance of the leaves. The genus comprises many pretty and elegant hardy annuals or perennials that are natives of northern temperate regions. The perennials are easily grown from seed or by cuttings of the young shoots taken in the spring, discarding the older woody central growth.

M. palustris (*scorpiodes*) (water forget-me-not) An attractive British native found growing in marshy ground by ponds and streams. The bright-blue flowers among the dark-green glossy foliage make this a most desirable plant for every water garden. Flowering freely during the spring and summer, it will grow either in mud at the edge of a pool or scrambling right into the water, and it will also

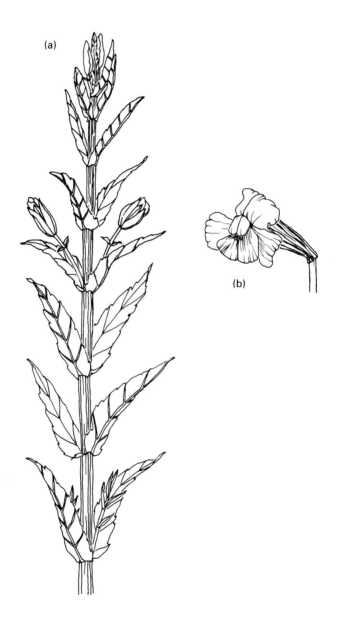

Flower Stem (a) and detached flower (b) of Mimulus ringens.

tolerate some shade. It is rather a vigorous spreader but it can be easily controlled by thinning out the many shoots in the spring or late summer. The variety *M. palustris* 'Mermaid' has larger and brighter flowers. Both grow to a height of 6–9in (15–22cm).

Myriophyllum (Order Haloragaceae)

M. proserpinacoides (parrot's feather)   A half-hardy aquatic which has most attractive feathery stems trailing and floating in shallow water. The tiny insignificant flowers are in whorls of five. It is easily grown in mud and shallow water and is a quick-spreading plant, but it will be destroyed by frosts. To prevent total losses a bowl of cuttings about 4–5in (12cm) long with a growing tip taken in July will soon root. Overwintered in a frost-free greenhouse or conservatory, the young plants will be ready to plant out the following spring.

Orontium (Order Araceae)

An old Greek name for a plant reputed to grow on the banks of the Syrian River Orontes.

O. aquaticum (golden club)   This is a handsome native of North America. Although a deep-rooted aquatic, it is one of the few that is non-invasive, growing best in water 6–15in (15–42cm) and in at least 12in (30cm) of soil. It is useless for growing in containers. In deep water the leaves, which are a metallic green above and silvery on the undersides, float on the water like small paddles, often a foot long. Flowering in May, the many narrow flower spikes protrude some 6–8in (15–20cm) out of the water similar to white candles studded with yellow florets, giving it a golden-tipped poker- or club-like appearance.

Peltandra (Order Araceae)

From the Greek *pelta*, a target or shield, and *andros*, a stamen, referring to the shape of the stamens. The genus comprises just two species of hardy aquatic perennials for growing in shallow water. They are natives of North America.

P. alba (white arrow arum)   A spectacular plant that is not often seen in water gardens. The arrow-shaped foliage is dark green and undulating. The white spathe is convulate with a shorter spadix similar to a *Calla*, only larger at 3–4in (7–10cm). It is in character during June. Clusters of red berries follow the flowers.

P. virginica (green arrow arum)   The best-known species in gardens. Succeeds in shallow water in a sunny sheltered situation. The large veined green leaves are sagittate and reach some two or more feet in length. Flowering in June, the greenish-yellow spathes are followed by clusters of globular green berries.

Pontederia (Order Pontederiaceae) (Pickerel Weed)

The genus is named after J. Pontedera (1688–1757), sometime Professor of Botany at Padua. One of the most popular aquatics that no water garden, large or small should be without. It is a most adaptable plant, thriving in water from between 3 and 6in (7–15cm) deep. It is perfectly hardy and can be propagated by division of the rootstocks in late spring or by seed sown as soon as it is ripe. A native of North America.

P. cordata   A handsome plant with sky-blue flowers and glossy green cordate (heart-shaped) leaves some 2ft (60cm) tall. Its compact and non-rampant growth makes it an ideal plant for all water gardens. For mass planting at the edge of the larger water garden and flowering in late summer and autumn it is unrivalled. It makes a striking contrast with *Lobelia speciosa* 'Queen Victoria', provided that this is growing in a damp border and not in the water.

P. lanceolata   The leaves of this variety are distinctly longer (*lanceolata* means 'lance-shaped') but cordate at the base. The bright-blue flowers, too, are longer and the overall plant grows to 4–5ft (1.2–1.5m). August–September flowering. Still comparatively rare.

Preslia (Order Labiatae)

A little-known aromatic plant related to *Mentha*, this is a hardy prostrate perennial thriving in mud or shallow water.

P. cevina   The single stems have narrow bract-like leaves with dense spikes of lavender-blue flowers. A dainty plant for the edge of the pool. There is a white form, *P. cevina alba*, which has creamy-white flowers. Summer-flowering. Both grow to 1ft (30cm).

Ranunculus (Order Ranunculaceae)

The name is Latin for a little frog, connoting the aquatic species of this large family.

R. flammula (lesser spearwort) The small golden-yellow flowers are barely ¾in (2cm) in diameter, with dark-green lanceolate leaves on prostrate or erect stems. It is a common British native plant found growing in marshes and ditches. Being much less invasive than the following species, this is a suitable plant for a wildlife pond.

R. lingua (greater spearwort) A handsome native to Britian with golden-yellow buttercup-like flowers up to 2in (5cm) in diameter on 2–3ft-high (60–90cm) hollow stems. The glossy lanceolate leaves are from 6 to 8in (15–20cm) long. The vigorous stoloniferous habit of this plant makes it totally unsuitable for garden ponds, and it should be planted only in confined areas of the larger water garden. Although it is spectacular, given a free root run it would soon colonize shallow water. *R. lingua* 'Grandiflora' is an improved form with larger flowers but just as vigorous.

Rumex (Order Polygonaceae)

The name is Latin for a dock. In the normal course of events it would be unthinkable to plant this coarse perennial but the following species can create a bold effect beside the larger water garden or lake.

R. hydrolapathum (great water dock) A vigorous perennial achieving 4–6ft-tall (1.2–1.8m) stems with dock-like leaves which assume fine autumnal tints of crimson. To prevent seedlings appearing the seed heads should be removed.

Sagittaria (Order Alismataceae) (Arrowhead)

Sagitta means an arrow and refers to the form of the leaves. This is another plant on which the botanists are at odds about the correct naming of the various clones available. The names listed first are the most common; newer or less well-known synonyms are in brackets. The genus comprises about fifteen species of greenhouse and hardy marsh-loving perennials, but only three are worthy of being considered for cultivation in the water garden. All have good architectural foliage. They will grow satisfactorily in water from 2 to 6in (5–15cm) deep.

S. japonica (*sagittifolia* var. *leucopetala*) (Japanese arrowhead)   This has large green arrow-shaped leaves. The three-petalled white flowers with green-yellow centres are in whorls on 2ft (60cm) stems.

S. japonica 'Flore Pleno' (*sagittifolia* var. *leucopetala* 'Flore Pleno') The handsome double form of the preceding species. The very double white flowers are in whorls and last longer. They are similar in appearance to a double stock with very distinctive large arrow-shaped leaves. Flowering in August, it grows to about 2ft (60cm). The rootstock is stoloniferous but much slower-growing than the preceding species. The tubers which are attached to the stolons are oval and are about the size of quails' eggs, and do not grow above the surface until about May or June. They may be sold as leafless tubers in early spring. If wild ducks are in the vicinity they seem to have an uncanny ability to locate dormant tubers in the mud of a pool and devour them with relish, usually during March.

S. sagittifolia (common arrowhead)   A native British aquatic found growing in watery ditches and beside pools. The three-petalled white flowers have purple-black centres and are similar in growth to the other species of the genus. Its stoloniferous habit is more vigorous and could become a nuisance unless controlled.

Saururus (Order *Saururaceae*) (*Lizard's Tail*)

The name comes from *sauros*, a lizard, and *oura*, a tail, referring to the form of the inflorescence. This small genus comprises just two species. Both are hardy aquatics. One is native of North America and the other is from eastern Asia. Only the first is in cultivation.

S. cernuus (American swamp lily)   The creamy-white flowers form a dense spike between 4 and 6in (10–15cm) long and nodding at the end (*cernuus* means 'drooping'). The fragrant flowers are complemented by attractive cordate foliage between 1 and 2ft high (30–60cm). June–August.

Scirpus (Order *Cyperaceae*)

Scirpus is Latin for a rush. This is a large genus, comprising hardy annual and perennial waterside plants. Of the many species that are found in Britain the best known is *S. lacustris*, which grows freely

Sagittaria japonica ‘Flore Pleno’ showing flower spike (a), leaf (b) and tuber (c).

in mud or shallow water. Easily increased by division of the suckers or rhizomes in spring. The other varieties may be similarly treated.

S. tabernaemontani 'Albescens'   A striking aquatic which has stout cylindrical rush-like foliage of sulphur white, contrasting with dark-green longitudinal stripes, which makes it a very conspicuous plant for the larger water garden. 4–5ft (1.2–1.5m).

S. lacustris (bulrush)   A handsome rush with dark-green cylindrical stems which attain a height of 5ft (1.5m) or more. The branched flower spikes are glabrous and red-brown in colour. They are in character during July–August. This plant was extensively used in making chair bottoms and mats in Britain and Europe.

S. tabernaemontani 'Zebrinus' (zebra rush)   Of Japanese origin, about 1881, this is an attractive ornamental rush with smooth stems banded with white and green in nearly equal tones, giving the appearance of a cluster of porcupine quills. Growing to a height of between 2 and 3ft (60–90cm), it is ideal for the smaller water garden. To maintain the distinctive stripes the plants require lifting every second spring and dividing, the outer portions being replanted in fresh soil.

Sparganium (Order Typhaceae) (Bur-Reed)

The name is derived from *sparganch*, a band, referring to the form of the leaves. A small genus of rather coarse marsh and aquatic plants which mostly inhabit the northern temperate regions, including Britain.

S. ramosum (erectum) (bede sedge)   This plant could be included in a planting scheme of a wildlife pond. The branched stems carry spiky globular inflorescences and were once used for making pepper.

Stachys (Order Labiatae) (Marsh Woundwort)

S. palustris   Another aquatic plant that should be planted only in a wildlife pond or a nature reserve on account of its rather weedy appearance. A native of the British Isles, it is usually found in watery ditches and muddy pools. The purplish flowers are in whorls on 3ft (1m) stems and the leaves are toothed, giving the appearance of a nettle.

Typha (Order Typhaceae) (Bulrush, Cat's Tail, Club Rush, Reedmace)

The old Greek name was used by Theophrastus. The many popular names describe just two of the most common British native aquatic plants thriving in ponds, lakes and watery ditches throughout the British Isles.

T. angustifolia (small bulrush or reed mace)   This is the more graceful of the two native species. The ¼–¾in-broad (0.6–1.8cm) dark-green leaves are channelled towards the base (*angustifolia* means narrow-leaved). The brown flower spikes are up to ¾in (1.8cm) in diameter and are on a monoecious spadix – that is, the male and female flowers are separated. The plant is in all parts smaller than *T. latifolia.*

T. latifolia (cat o'nine tails, marsh beetle, reedmace)   A plant of a robust constitution growing to between 5 and 8ft (1.5–2.5m) in height, the leaves from 4 to 6ft (1.2–2m) long and up to 1½in (4cm) wide (*latifolia* means broad-leaved). The dark-brown flower spikes which can be from 6in (15cm) extending to nearly 12in (30cm) long and an inch in diameter are almost contiguous. They are in character from July and last well into the autumn. Both *T. latifolia* and *T. angustifolia* are fine for naturalizing in lakes but on account of the vigorous stoloniferous root system they are unsuitable for growing in garden ponds.

T. laxmannii (T. stenophyllus)   This is a much more slender plant at 3–4ft (0.9–1.2m) high. The dark-green semi-cylindrical leaves are very narrow. The slim brown flower spike is similar in character to the aforegoing species. A native of south-east Europe.

T. minima   This is a real miniature. The grassy foliage grows only to 1–1½ft (30–45cm) and, with almost circular dark-brown inflorescences about 1in (2.5cm) in diameter, makes this plant ideal for garden ponds and tub culture – it requires only 1–2in (2.5–5cm) of water. A native of eastern Europe, it is perfectly hardy. *T. laxmannii* and *T. minima* are the only species that are suitable for growing in garden ponds.

Veronica (Order Scrophulariaceae) (Brooklime)

V. beccabunga   The only aquatic member of this genus of otherwise herbaceous plants. It is found growing in watery ditches and marshy ground throughout the British Isles. Although it may be considered a rather weedy aquatic, it is worth growing on account of its glossy green prostrate foliage on creeping stems and bright-blue flowers. Trim back any stems that have outgrown their allocated space.

Zantedeschia (Order Araceae)

Z. aethiopica (white arum, trumpet lily, lily of the Nile) The old botanical name, *Richardia aethiopica*, was given in honour of L. C. Richard (1754–1821), an eminent French botanist. This is a well-known genus of greenhouse or nearly hardy marsh-loving perennials from South Africa with thick rhizomes and large shiny leaves. The plant is adapted for growing under glass in 3-litre pots containing a rich compost and kept watered copiously. They made admirable subjects for the conservatories that were so popular in Victorian times. In the summer they can be lowered in their pots into the pond to continue flowering. Remove them to frost-free quarters for the resting period in winter. If the plants are to remain in the water over the winter, then provide at least 6in (15cm) of water over the crowns to prevent the rootstock from freezing. It has beautiful white spathes with bright-yellow spadices growing to about 2–2½ft (60–75cm). The dark-green sagittate leaves are about half as broad as they are long and are borne on long petioles.

Z. aethiopica 'Crowborough' This variety was found growing in a garden in Crowborough, Sussex, England, in the 1950s. It is almost identical to the above-named except that this has proved a hardy border plant after an initial period of two or three seasons to become established. Until then, protect it from frost with straw or litter. The mature roots will find their way to a great depth. It will also grow perfectly well in water, where it will make an arresting feature in the garden pool. Propagation is by division and by the many suckers that are produced, which can be potted up separately and grown on. This is best done in the spring.

MARGINAL AQUATIC PLANTS AT A GLANCE

I have selected twelve of the best marginal plants which are the most suitable for garden ponds of all sizes and for growing in water from 2 to 4in (5–10cm) deep.

Acorus calamus 'Variegatus' (variegated sweet flag) Pink, white and cream foliage. 2–3ft (60–90cm).

Nymphaea 'Mrs Richmond'.

Nymphaea 'James Brydon'.

Nymphaea 'Gladstoniana'. The best white for the largest pond or lake.

Nymphaea 'Sunrise'. A very fine lily that is still comparatively rare.

Nymphaea 'Comanche'. The large flowers open as pale yellow passing to warm coppery-red with age.

Zantedechia aethiopica 'Crowborough'. This is hardy if it is submerged below the ice level of the pond.

Scirpus zebrinus. The zebra rush.

Iris pseudacorus 'Variegata'. A very striking spring foliage plant.

Mimulus cupreus. Thrives best in a very watery situation.

Caltha palustris 'Plena'. The double marsh marigold.

Astilbe 'White Gloria'.

Astilbe 'Montgomery'. Probably the darkest red astilbe in cultivation.

Matteuccia struthiopteris or *Struthiopteris germanica.* The ostrich feather fern. It needs ample moisture to do well.

Hemerocallis multiflorus. A very useful late-flowering day-lily. The small flowers are on branched stems.

Iris sibirica 'Perry's Blue'. An old variety but still worthy of cultivation. It is seen here growing in a damp border beside a formal pool.

Lobelia speciosa 'Queen Victoria'.   Well-grown plants will reach 5ft (150cm). Never grow lobelias in water.

Dactylorhiza latifolia (marsh orchid).   Easily grown in a damp peaty soil.

Gunnera manicata.   Seen growing beside a natural pond.

Primula japonica 'Postford White'. This comes more or less true from seed if it is widely separated from others.

Trollius ledebourii 'Golden Queen'.   A useful midsummer-flowering *Trollius*.

Butomus umbellatus (flowering rush) Rose-pink flowers on 3ft (90cm) stems. July–August.

Calla palustris (bog arum) A creeping plant, ideal for masking the edges of concrete or fibreglass ponds.

Caltha palustris (marsh marigold) This and the next species are best grown in mud or just an inch of water.

Caltha palustris 'Plena' (double marsh marigold).

Iris pseudacorus 'Variegatus' Gold and green foliage in early summer. Yellow flowers.

Iris laevigata (Japanese water iris) Not to be confused with *Iris kaempferi*. *I. laevigata* has blue flowers.

Iris laevigata 'Albo-purpurea' Has blue flowers flecked white.

Myosotis palustris (water forget-me-not) This plant may spread mildly but not so much as to become a nuisance.

Pontederia cordata (pickerel weed) A useful late-summer-flowering aquatic with blue flowers. 2ft (60cm).

Sagittaria japonica 'Flore pleno' (double arrowhead)

Scirpus 'Zebrinus' (zebra rush) Horizontally striped rush.

The following marginal plants, in addition to those already highlighted, are also ideal for planting in the margins of larger ponds and natural lakes.

Caltha polypetala (giant marsh marigold).

Iris pseudacorus (yellow flag iris).

Orontium aquaticum (golden club) Needs a deep soil and from 6in to 1ft (15–30cm) of water to do well.

Ranunculus lingua 'Grandiflorus' (greater spearwort) If you are prepared to keep this plant within its allotted territory, it can be a fine feature beside a lake. It is not suitable for garden ponds.

Scirpus 'Albescens' Stout sulphur-white stems, 4–6ft (1.2–1.8m) high.

Scirpus lacustris Dark-green cylindrical stems.

Typha angustifolia Narrow-leaved reedmace.

Alisma species Attractive enough, but the abundance of seed that is produced readily germinates unless the flower heads are cut off before the seed has set.

Some aquatics to beware of on account of their invasive nature.

Eriophorum Strong growing and best seen growing in natural acid bogs.

Glyceria aquatica 'Variegata' Too invasive for most garden ponds, but can be effective beside a lake or large pond, provided that it can be kept under control

Ranunculus lingua 'Grandiflorus' This has been mentioned before as a plant capable of covering a garden pond in a very short time.

Sparganium ramosum (erectum) Too invasive for most ponds but it could be included with caution in a wildlife pond.

Typha latifolia Very invasive. This has been known to puncture plastic pool liners. *T. angustifolia* is less of a problem.

6
PESTS AND DISEASES

It would be something of a miracle if water plants, and water lilies, in particular were immune from attacks by any sort of pest or disease. Unfortuately, though, they are as prone to them as all other garden plants. However, most can be successfully controlled without the use of chemicals, through prudent management of the water garden. Ornamental fish are the natural enemy of these predators and no garden pond should be without its quota.

WATER LILY BEETLE

The water lily beetle (*Galeruella nymphaeae*) is one of the most destructive pests of the water garden. Fortunately, it rarely occurs in garden ponds, but in lakes and large ponds control could be more difficult. By channelling and feeding on the foliage, during the course of a season the beetles will reduce the lily pads to a brown and crinkled mass. Some water lilies are especially selected for attack, in particular N. × *marliacea* 'Albida'.

Clusters of about twenty yellowish eggs are laid by the adult beetle in late spring on the upper side of the leaves and within a week or so they hatch out into small wrinkled black grubs with a distinctive orange belly. They then begin to feed on the leaf tissue, causing a network of channels. After they are fully fed they pupate on the leaves and then hatch into the adult beetle. There are normally two generations a year and all stages of the insect can be seen on the leaves together. During the autumn the beetle goes into hibernation in nearby rushes and in hollow stems of plants.

Control is best effected by washing the larvae off the lily pads into the water with a strong jet from a hose. The fish will then devour them. In severe infestations the leaves should be removed and burned. During the autumn, cut down rushes and all nearby waterside herbaceous plants close to the ground and burn without delay.

WATER LILY APHIDS

Water lily aphids can be disposed of in the same way. Dislodge them into the water so that the fish can devour them. They are their natural food. This pest infests various water plants. It is more prevalent on plants under glass but nevertheless it can be a problem, particularly in a hot dry summer. In heavy infestations the pest can completely spoil the appearance of flowers, stems and foliage. It is usually seen from June onwards. In the autumn they migrate to tree hosts, especially plum trees and blackthorn, where the overwintering eggs are laid. The winged females migrate to water lilies in the summer.

BROWN CHINA-MARKS MOTH

The lava of the brown china-marks moth is a curious but interesting pest. It sometimes attacks the leaves of water lilies and other aquatic plants, feeding on the leaves and in severe cases reducing the foliage to a ragged and rotting mass. The eggs are laid by the adult moth in small clusters near the edge or on the underside of the leaf. In due course these hatch out into creamy coloured worms or larvae about ¾–1in (2–2.5cm) long. They have a distinctive brown line running down the back and a brown head. The larva is found throughout the summer months living inside a flat case made of two oval pieces of leaf fastened together at the sides with silk. It is able to move about and feed protected inside the case but sometimes as the larva grows it will make itself a larger case to accommodate its extra size. The larvae eventually pupate, forming silken cocoons within their protected case on the water plant. About three to four weeks later a small but perfect brown and white moth emerges from the cocoon.

Although water lilies are the most vulnerable to attack by this pest, it also attacks *Aponogeton*, *Alisma plantago* and *Hydrocharis morsus-ranae*. In small ponds the larvae can be removed relatively easily by hand but a larger infestation is best dealt with by flooding and submerging the foliage so that the larvae are either eaten by fish or are drowned.

IRIS SAWFLY

The larvae of the iris sawfly are active during the summer months eating the leaf margins of waterside irises to produce a ragged or even a serrated effect. When fully fed they pupate in the soil and the adults emerge in the following spring. Insecticides such as malathion or liquid derris which are suitable for controlling the pests should not be used where fish are present. It would therefore be prudent to hand-pick the larvae and cut down the unsightly foliage.

BLOODWORMS

Bloodworms are found in most garden pools. They are the larvae of midges and are about ½–1in (1–2.5cm) long and blood-red in colour. Although they feed on decayed vegetation at the bottom of the pool they are often to be seen writhing awkwardly through the water in a series of figure-of-eights. Some water lilies – especially the yellow varieties N. × *marliacea* 'Chromatella', N. 'Moorei' and N. *pygmaea* 'Helvola' – are subject to attack by these bloodworms, particularly any part of the root or stem that happens to be in the process of rotting through natural causes. I am, however, convinced that these worms are not the sole cause of a complete water lily dying. Lift a suspect plant and it will be noticed that a knot of these worms will be attached to the root. Trim back the foliage and roots and wash the plant in a solution of liquid derris as directed by the manufacturers. Leave it in the solution for a few minutes before rinsing in fresh water and replanting. Liquid derris is poisonous to fish. A pond with an adequate number of fish should keep these bloodworms in check as they form an important food supply for them.

IRIS FLEABEETLE

The iris fleabeetle occasionally occurs in large numbers in mid-summer, attacking waterside irises. They are bright blue and are similar to the fleabeetles that are sometimes seen in the vegetable garden attacking members of the brassica family. But their feeding habits differ. Instead of peppering the leaves with tiny round holes, like the brassica fleabeetle, small longitudinal areas become devoid of leaf tissue and give the appearance of a leaf skeleton. Where there is no danger of contaminating ponds containing fish, spraying with DDT will control the pests; otherwise, trim back affected foliage and burn.

CADDIS FLIES

Caddis flies belong to the order Trichoptera and are small moth-like insects except that the wings are clothed with hairs instead of scales. They lay their eggs near the water. The larvae (known as stick grubs) live in the water and make portable shelters out of sand, stones or plant fragments. They can do a great deal of damage in the process by biting through the roots, stems or flower buds of aquatic plants. If fish are present, particularly golden orfe, they should deal adequately with the situation.

WATER LILY LEAF SPOT

Water lily leaf spot is caused by the fungus *Ovularia nymaearum*. The rounded spots when first noticed are a reddish colour, changing to enlarged dark-brown or black patches and eventually rotting. The affected leaves should be removed and burnt.

WATER LILY CROWN ROT

Water lily crown rot is caused by a species of the fungus *Phytopthora*. The trouble shows itself with the yellowing of the leaves of the plant, the stems becoming brittle and breaking from the crown until finally the plant is reduced to an evil-smelling black rotting mass. There is no known cure for this disease so the infected lily roots must be removed and destroyed. The pool itself should be sterilized with disinfectant after the removal of all other aquatic plants and, of course, fish to temporary quarters. As a precaution against this fungal disease, some commercial growers dip all incoming or propagated water lily root stocks in a solution of Aaterra as recommended by the manufacturers in the United Kingdom. The chemical Banrot is used in the USA. The varieties of water lilies that are most susceptible are the yellow and copper shades, although no variety is completely immune.

GREEN WATER

One of the most distressing sights to see soon after the completion of a garden pond is the appearance of green water, often the forerunner of blanketweed or algae. The water first becomes cloudy and more opaque and then turns green or reddish-brown. In established ponds the water is usually clear for most of the year, but sometimes long filamentous strands of blanketweed cling to the plants and sides of ponds or just float aimlessly about.

We need to know why this should occur and what measures should be adopted for prevention or cure.

Green water appearing in a newly built pond is a perfectly natural phenomenon. It is caused by millions of microscopic airborne spores that arrive within a week or so of the water being introduced. These then become suspended in the water where, under the influence of light, they will grow and multiply, feeding on the dissolved mineral salts in the water (usually tap water) and, as the soil breaks down, on the fresh minerals that are released. All this encourages the algae to spread. Shallow pools where the water can be abnormally warm, an abundance of fresh manure or too much artificial fertilizer and direct sunlight are recipes for green water and blanketweed to flourish.

However, it is important for a successful water garden to be in a sheltered site and exposed to full sunlight. The biggest and most important competitor to algae is other aquatic plants which will grow and provide the necessary shade in order to starve the algae of food and light.

Pond plants should be planted in good fibre-free loam, with water lilies, whose leaves help to exclude light, marginal plants, which create competition with the green water for food and, most important of all, oxygenating plants used in conjunction with floating aquatics. Once these settle in and grow, the water will become clear. The initial green water or scum can easily be removed from a small pool simply by drawing a sheet of newspaper across the water. In larger pools disturbing the water by means of a hose is a satisfactory method.

A layer of washed pea shingle acts as a top dressing to all aquatic plantings and this will prevent fish from stirring up the mud.

If blanketweed becomes twisted round the plants, it is best to remove it by hand. A lawn rake is a useful tool for removing the algae from the centre of a pool. Avoid throwing the algae down at the pool side but collect it up and consign it to the compost heap. Persevere with this task for a while and you should be on the winning side. There is no advantage in changing the water in order to rid the pool of green water.

I have never advocated the use of any of the chemicals that are on the market, although most now claim that they are perfectly harmless to fish. Provided that you use the correct soil and an adequate number of oxygenating and floating plants the water will eventually clear.

BLACK VINE WEEVIL

Although not an aquatic pest, the black vine weevil is causing increasing concern amongst nurserymen specializing in hardy container-grown nursery stock. Among the many shrubs, vines and plants that it attacks are a number of waterside perennials – rodgersias, primulas, astilbes and hostas. In fact almost any terrestrial plant is vulnerable. Hitherto it was principally confined to glass-house crops and in particular cyclamen and begonias, but the pest was easily controlled simply by incorporating aldrin into the compost. Under recent Common Market regulations this chemical is no longer available in the EEC.

Purchasing container-grown stock from garden centres requires a keen eye to identify the symptoms of attack. The first signs to watch for are semicircular segments eaten from the margins of the leaves by the adult beetle. You are unlikely to see the wingless black beetles as they are nocturnal feeders, crawling back into the soil during the day.

The adult beetle, which is a little under ½in (1.5cm) long, lays up to 500 eggs in the soil near the host plant. They hatch out in two or three weeks. The larvae feed upon the roots until fully grown and then burrow into the soil to pupate. The plant then begins to take on a wilting effect and on closer examination it will be found that almost the entire root system has been eaten away, leaving the rootless plant sitting on the soil.

As for controlling these pests, there are various materials that can be used as a drench. Gamma HCH has been successful. Examining the plants for the large, slow-moving weevils and then treading on them is an effective method of control. Outdoor birds such as the song-thrush can often give some natural control.

MOLLUSCS

Pond snails are often recommended as essential for garden ponds. To a certain degree this is true. They feed on decaying vegetation and a certain amount of algae, though the effect is practically negligible.

There are two species to consider for garden ponds. First is the great pond snail, *Limnea stagnalis*. These are prolific breeders; too many will not only feed on the decayed vegetation but will also consume young aquatic growths. The egg clusters are easily recognizable as inch-long oblong-shaped spawn attached to the underside of the lily pad. Very often water lilies are bought with snail spawn already attached to part of the foliage. One way to reduce the numbers is to place a cabbage stump and leaf on to the surface of the water overnight. The following morning the leaf will have collected a surprising number of snails. Repeat for several nights if necessary.

Planorbis corneus, the black ramshorn snail, is a much more desirable occupant of the pond and should not be considered a pest. In this species the egg clusters that are laid on the underside of the leaves are circular. The snails spend most of their time clinging to the side of the pond, feeding on the short lengths of algae as well as some decayed vegetation. *Planorbis corneus* are air breathers but come to the surface because the body contains haemoglobin and can absorb oxygen from the water. There is also a red ramshorn, *Planorbis corneus rubra*, which is comparatively rare. Both *Planorbis* species are interesting and are suitable for ponds and slow-running streams.

LARGER CREATURES

Water rats are occasionally found in the banks of large natural ponds and lakes, where they will eat the flowers, often taking them to the bank to enjoy at their leisure. Trapping or shooting seems to be the only method of destroying them.

Waterhens, or moorhens, can be just as destructive to water lilies and other aquatic plants, reducing them to mere shreds. During the spring the waterhens will build their nests in secluded clumps of rushes or *Caltha polypetala*. These birds, however, must not be destroyed but the plants should be protected with netting.

Other livestock found in ponds includes the great diving beetle, the water boatman and the whirligig beetle. These are carnivorous aquatic insects and so do not come within the scope of this book.

7
THE BOG GARDEN

Defining a bog garden can be a little difficult. I must therefore be precise and state exactly the moisture requirements of the plants described.

To many gardeners a bog means a peaty soil, squelchy to walk on and very acid 3–4 on the pH scale. Bogs of this kind, which took 10,000 years to form, are habitats of specialized bog plants such as *Drosera* spp (sundews), *Eriophorum* spp (cotton grass) and a number of bog orchids, but in recent years there has been a growing concern at how fast the peat of these is being extracted for use in the horticultural industry. In the United Kingdom, the commercial sphagnum peat extraction is carried out mainly in the Lowlands of Scotland, the Welsh borders and the north of England. Sedge peat is extracted in the Somerset levels. Present estimates indicate that existing peat reserves are likely to disappear within twenty years. Environmentalists are now calling on the government to carry out research into alternative growing materials for the horticultural industry, and to encourage gardeners to use bark or compost wherever possible. After all, peat is not a plant food, as the environmentalists point out. Kitchen waste composted with lawn mowings, straw and annual weeds (not perennials – they must be burnt) makes a very suitable alternative as a top dressing for plants and shrubs.

I make the point about peat bogs simply because so often the first ingredient to be bought from the garden centre is a bale or two of the peat to provide the basis of a bog garden. We have now become aware that there are alternatives for enriching an otherwise dryish soil or for improving moisture retention, so I can now proceed to describe the different types of bog garden and the most suitable plants to complement a garden pond.

The banks of a stream or natural pool, however, will be quite different. Here the ground can be rich and deep, containing silt and humus. This situation is perfect for growing the widest range of waterside plants. Plant those that prefer slightly dryer conditions farther away from the water, while those that are more suited to wetter conditions can be placed nearer the water and, of course, the true aquatics in the water itself. Note carefully any rise and fall in the water level. Plants such as *Astilbe*, *Rheum* and *Trollius* like a damp situation in the spring and summer but any lengthy period of waterlogging during the winter would rot the rootstocks of most.

Before any sort of planting can be undertaken thorough preparation of the soil is of the utmost importance, particularly as any existing perennial weeds in the banks of natural streams or ponds are usually of a tough and uncompromising nature. Removing them by hand usually means removing a larger than normal amount of wet soil. This need not necessarily be a problem as the replacement can be garden compost, provided that it is well rotted and weed-free. Treating badly affected areas with glyphosate (Tumbleweed) is usually very effective but care must be taken not to let any spray drift into the water. A second application may be necessary about two months later to kill off any particularly stubborn weeds. These applications are best applied in late spring and summer. Follow the maker's instructions to the letter.

Sometimes it may be possible to cover a particularly weedy area with black polythene. Make sure that the edges are secure by placing a layer of soil round the perimeter. This also prevents any light from entering. This should kill most weeds within a few months. For best results this should be done during the summer.

A natural stream or a naturally boggy area with an unusually high proportion of perennial weeds can be a daunting proposition for those wishing to make use of this highly desirable natural asset. The question that is often asked is when is the best time to tackle the job. Assuming that the area in question is manageable by one person and that only hand tools are available, autumn is much the best time, simply because from a gardener's point of view this is the least busy time of year. In spring you are at your busiest and in summer it is often too hot to contemplate any heavy digging. Dig the soil over and leave it in a rough state for the winter rain and frost to break it down. In spring the soil can be broken down still further, and any visible weeds removed. Alternatively, if the ground is naturally boggy to the point of saturation, it may be easier and appropriate simply to remove the weeds without digging. Turning over wet clods of soil could be extremely difficult as well as undesirable. It depends on the situation. In any case, the perennial weeds must be removed before planting can take place. Leaving the ground fallow over the summer would be beneficial: any weeds that germinate can either be dug up or sprayed with glyphosphate (choose a still summer evening). By the autumn conditions should be suitable for the initial planting.

Creating an artificial bog garden is a relatively easy operation by comparison, provided that some important points are observed. Such a garden provides the completeness an informal pool so often needs.

The soil immediately adjacent to an artificial pool is often quite dry – in fact too dry to accommodate any sort of bog-garden plant. To create a boggy or marshy area, first mark out the area required and excavate to a depth of not less than 12in (30cm), and then place a sheet of polythene (500-gauge is ideal) in the excavation. Fill with a layer of coarse-chopped fibrous turf followed by a layer of well-rotted farmyard manure. If manure is unobtainable, use well-rotted compost mixed with the topsoil that was excavated. Leave this for a few weeks to settle, after which it may be necessary to top up with a further layer of compost. Allow a further settling period before planting.

WATERSIDE PLANTS

The following list of plants represents a wide range of waterside perennials suitable for growing in constantly boggy or very wet soil or humus-rich soil that does not dry out. Generally speaking, plants suitable for damp woodland conditions only are not included. Obviously, there are some that would overlap in this category – plants which are perfectly happy in full sun provided that they are growing in a wet situation and those which tolerate partial shade and are less reliant on moisture.

Aconitum (Order Ranunculaceae) (Monkshood, Wolfbane)

Not often considered as water-garden plants, these species do nevertheless require a rich, moisture-retentive soil and are invaluable for growing beneath the shade of trees. The native British species, *A. anglicum*, the only *Aconitum* to flower in the spring, is found in shady damp spots beside woodland streams. All are easily propagated, either by division in the early spring (take care not to leave any piece of the root about for these are very poisonous) or from seed sown as soon as ripe in the open or in a cold frame.

There are several excellent varieties for flowering during the summer. *A.* 'Arendsii' has amethyst-blue hooded flowers in late summer and grows taller than most at 4–5ft (1.2–1.5m). 'Bicolor' has blue and white flowers on branching stems. 'Blue Sceptre' has similar flowers and 'Bressingham Spire' has violet-blue flowers. Both of these have tall straight stems to 3ft (1m). 'Sparks Variety', sometimes known as *henryi*, is another with deep-violet-blue flowers. Tall-growing at 4–5ft (1.2–1.5m) and with a long flower season, it would make a striking contrast with the yellow day lilies.

Actaea (Order Ranunculaceae) (Baneberry)

A small genus of hardy herbaceous plants with long racemes of fluffy white flowers followed by white or red poisonous berries. They grow best in a rich, moisture-retentive soil and light shade from trees or shrubs. *A. alba* (white baneberry) has finely cut green leaves with spikes that top the foliage with pure white poisonous berries in late summer. *A. rubra* is similar but with crimson berries, equally poisonous. Both are native to North America. *A. spicata*, a native of Britain and known as herb Christopher, is similar to the North American species except that the berries are black. All these grow to about 18in (45cm) and enjoy similar growing conditions. Propagation is by seed.

Ajuga (Order Labiatae) (Bugle)

Low-growing herbaceous perennial plants requiring a damp soil in sun or part shade. They are usually procumbent and sometimes stoloniferous, which makes them useful subjects for carpeting areas in a frontal position of a border. *A. reptans* (creeping) is a native of the British Isles and is found growing in moist areas beside streams and in wetlands. There are several dark-leaved and variegated forms superior to the species. *A. reptans* 'Burgundy Glow' has green, crimson and blotched cream foliage and pale-blue spikes only 4in (10cm) high. *A. reptans purpurea* is reddish-purple with similar blue flowers. Both thrive best in moist soil, sun or part shade.

Anemone (Order Ranunculaceae) (Wind Flower)

The name comes from *anemos*, wind; the greater part of this large and diverse family grow in elevated places much exposed to the wind. Only a very few are for inclusion in the bog garden. *A. rivularis*, a native of north India, is quite hardy and favours a rich, moisture-retentive soil in sun or partial shade. The villose divided foliage and 2ft-high (60cm) branched stems give rise to white flowers whose sepals are stained violet-blue and purple anthers within. It flowers from late spring to early summer.

Aruncus (Order Rosaceae) (Goatsbeard)

A. aethusifolius   A delightful Japanese dwarf goatsbeard with finely divided foliage. Short spikes of dull white flowers on reddish stems. Compact habit in a rich moist soil. Division of the rootstock in spring.

A. sylvester (dioicus)   A handsome plant for the damp parts of the water garden or in the wild garden, in rich soil, sun or part shade. Tall stems, often 6ft (2m) or more, are clothed with creamy-white spiraea-like plumes in midsummer. Good green pinnately divided foliage. In spring this is often bronze-green. Propagation can be a difficult task if you attempt to lift an established clump. It has just about the toughest rootstock of any herbaceous plant so raising plants from seed is the most satisfactory method, particularly from the female plant which has the more ornamental seed heads. The male plants produce few if any seed but the plumes are more feathery in appearance.

A. sylvester 'Kneiffii'   More suited for the smaller garden but requiring the same conditions. Very finely divided foliage with graceful creamy-white plumes on 2ft (60cm) stems.

Astilbe (Order Saxifragaceae)

The letter *a* means 'without' and *stilbe*, 'brilliance' – an allusion to the inconspicuous flowers of some of the species. The word *Astilbe* was inspired by Buchanan-Hamilton in 1825 but published by D. Don in 1834 and explained by his brother G. Don. A genus of about a dozen species that originate mainly from Japan and other areas of Asia. From a tough rootstock grow flower stems from 6in (15cm) to 6ft (2m) long, widely branching and tapering in panicles. The leaves are triternate or biternate (in threes or twos), unrelated to spiraea, which they are still erroneously sometimes called. The astilbes are graceful and indispensable hardy herbaceous plants for the water garden, thriving in a rich soil that is constantly moist in the summer. Most are better in light or partial shade. This is particularly true with those of a magenta colour where the green foliage from the trees and shrubs, providing the shade, softens the harshness of colour. The delicate foliage of the early-flowering hybrids and species is vulnerable to late spring frosts. However, these astilbes make fine subjects for forcing in gentle heat or just cold glass for a spring display.

The modern conservatories built in the Victorian style which are now so popular lend themselves to these once-popular plants. Some nurseries still offer large clumps specially for forcing, but not all varieties are suitable. The clumps can be potted into 6in (15cm) or 3-litre pots from November until February. Use a rich compost and keep them well watered. This method will provide a fine display during May. They were once displayed so superbly at many Chelsea flower shows by Bees of Chester. The species readily set seed which germinates freely, but the named hybrids can be propagated only by division of the rootstock, preferably in the spring just before growth starts.

Using just four *Astilbe* species, two Continental hybridists put their skills to the test and produced an unrivalled range of the modern astilbe hybrids known today as *A.* × *arendsii*. Lemoine of Nancy, France, pioneered the work and Georg Arends of Ronsdorf, Germany, continued by crossing the Chinese species *A. davidii*, rosy magenta, with the white *A. astilboides*. The resultant hybrids were in various shades of lilac and rose. A further cross with the white *A. japonica* gave white, pink and salmon shades and finally a cross with *A. thunbergii* gave rise to the taller varieties in varying shades of pink and white. Further crosses have given us more first-rate hybrids with colours ranging from pure white, cream and pink to salmon to carmine and deep red.

With such a range of colour and diversity of form there can be few herbaceous plants that are more rewarding than astilbes, provided that they are given their essential requirements. They will not tolerate waterlogging in the winter, which causes rotting of the rootstock, but they can remain for many years in the same position provided that a spring mulch of compost is applied and an application of a general fertilizer sprinkled around the plants. Planting of bare root plants can take place at any time between October and March; container-grown plants can be planted at any time.

I have listed an extensive range of these most desirable plants with detailed descriptions which will enable you to select the most suitable kinds for your own water garden or herbaceous border. The first to be listed are the species which have now become quite rare.

Astilbe astilboides   A Japanese species that has white flowers in dense spikes some 2–3ft (60–90cm) high. June flowering.
A. chinensis (China, 1892)   The hybrid 'Pumila' is dwarf at between 6 and 12in (15–30cm), with tapering stiff spikes of mulberry-red flowers. The rootstock is of a creeping habit, which

makes this variety a very useful ground-cover plant in a moist shady spot on the edge of the border. Later flowering than most, in August.

A. × *crispa* A group of hybrids with distinctive crinkled bronze-green foliage. Stumpy bright magenta flowers during July. 9in (22.5cm) high. Slow-growing. *A.* × *crispa* 'Perkeo' is the best known.

A. davidii The almost magenta lilac flowers are borne in loose panicles. This species grows from 4 to 6ft (1.2–2m), according to soil conditions, and is later than most. It is a parent of many hybrids; a notable one is *A. taquettii* 'Superba'.

A. japonica (Japan) Small pure white flowers in large racemose panicles. It flowers early in May and is subject to late spring frosts but is a useful plant for forcing under glass. 2ft (60cm).

A. koreana (Korea) Arching sprays with rose-pink buds opening out to creamy-white inflorescences in midsummer. This species is not so dependent on moisture as others.

A. rivularis An imposing plant, best suited for the margins of lakes or deep woodlands. The 6ft-high (2m) slightly arching stems carry greenish-white flowers. Superb deeply divided foliage. It is one of the few astilbes that spread with underground shoots, but is easily controlled with the use of a spade to cut them back.

A. rubra A particularly rare species with numerous rose-pink flowers in dense panicles in late summer. Glossy foliage.

A. thunbergii Earlier flowering than the other species, with many small white flowers in branched pyramidal panicles with reddish and slightly downy stalks. Sharply toothed yellowish foliage. A parent of many hybrids. *A.* 'Ostrich Plume' is a well-known rose-pink variety and both grow to about 3ft (1m).

A. simplicifolia The true plant is a dwarf, growing to only 4–5in (10–12cm) high. Deeply cut or lobed glossy foliage with small slender branches of pale-pink flowers. A gem for a damp spot in the rock garden.

The astilbes that are most usually seen and those that are generally available from garden centres and nurseries are listed below. The medium and tall garden hybrids are invaluable for waterside planting in association with candelabra primulas, *Iris sibirica* and *Trollius*. If you choose the earliest-flowering varieties through to the latest, a very long season can be enjoyed. Plant about 1½–2ft (45–60cm) apart according to height. The flowering season begins in June for the earliest kinds.

White Varieties

(F) indicates varieties suitable for forcing.

'Deutschland' (Arends, 1920)   Sheaves of ivory white, with green leaves. Mid-season. 2ft (60cm).
'Irrlicht' (Theoboldt, 1939) (F)   Pure-white flowers on tapered spikes fading to green with age. Good dark-bronze-purple foliage. This variety is used extensively for forcing. Early. 2ft (60cm).
'Professor Van der Wielen' (Ruys, 1917) Of *thunbergii* parentage. Large drooping spikes with ample green foliage. This variety is more suitable beside larger ponds and lakes. Mid-season. 4ft (1.2m).
'White Gloria' (Arends, 1924) (F)   Dense spikes of creamy-white flowers. Compact with dark-green foliage. Early. 2ft (60cm).

Pink Varieties

'Betsy Cuperus' (Ruys, 1917)   One of the finest for the larger border. Stout full spikes, terminating with drooping sprays of pure-white flowers with pink centres. Mid-season. 4–5ft (1.2–1.5m).
'Bressingham Beauty' (Bloom)   Free-flowering with spikes of rich pink. Mid-season. 3ft (90cm).
'Ceres' (Arends, 1909)   An early hybrid with pale-pink flowers in open sprays. 3ft (1m). Mid- to late-season.
'Finale' (Arends, 1952)   A *chinensis* hybrid with feathery pink flowers late in the season. 1½–2ft (45–60cm).
'Ostrich Plume' (Arends, 1952)   'Straussenfeder' of *thunbergii* parentage. Distinctive arching sprays of bright pink. Glossy green foliage. Mid- to late-season. 3ft (1m).
'Rhineland' (Arends, 1920) (F)   Bright-pink dense plumes, bushy habit. 2ft (60cm). Early.
'Venus' (Arends, 1910)   Strong-growing, with tall spikes of rosy-pink flowers. 4ft (1.2m). Mid- to late season.

Red Varieties

'Amethyst' (Arends, 1920)   Open spikes of lilac purple. 3ft (90cm). Mid-season.
'Cologne' (Arends, 1930) (F)   Deep carmine-rose, compact growth and free-flowering. 2ft (60cm). Early.
'Fanal' (Arends, 1933) (F)   Intense dark-red plumes over mounded dark foliage. Reliable and free. Low-growing at only 1½ft (45cm). Mid-season.

'Federsee' (Theoboldt, 1939) (F)   Bright rosy-red plumes, distinctive coppery-coloured foliage. This variety is adaptable to drier conditions than most. Mid-season. 2ft (60cm).

'Fire' ('Feuer') (Arends, 1940)   Aptly named, with intense salmon-red feathery spikes. 2ft (60cm). Mid-season to late.

'Glow' ('Glut') (Arends, 1952)   This is an even deeper colour, a glowing ruby red with dark foliage. 2ft (60cm). Mid-season to late.

'Jo Ophurst' (Ruys, 1916)   Dense upright spikes of ruby red. 3ft (90cm). Late.

'Montgomery' (Kooy, 1949)   Possibly the darkest red of all. 2ft (60cm). Early to mid-season.

'Salland' (Ruys, 1913)   Slender spikes of carmine rose. One of the tallest astilbes and suitable for only the large water garden or border. 6ft (2m) Late.

'Serenade' (Arends, 1954)   Tapering spikes of deep rosy lilac. 2ft (60cm). Late.

'Spinell' (Arends, 1955)   Feathery red plumes. Deserves to be better known. 3ft (90cm). Mid-season.

Simplicifolia Hybrids or Dwarf Hybrids

This group is the result of hybridizing *A. simplicifolia* with possibly *A. chinensis* and *A. japonica*. Chiefly the work of Georg Arends. These quite delightful astilbes make attractive groups beside the small pool, water garden or stream side, preferring the same conditions as their taller relatives. However, they do flower a little later than most, extending the flowering season well into August.

A. simplicifolia 'Alba' (Arends, 1923)   In spite of its name, it is a very pale shell-pink in 12in (30cm) plumes.

'Aphrodite' (Pagels, 1958)   Deep pink. Glossy dark foliage. 15in (38cm).

'Atrorosea' (Arends, 1954)   Bold plumes of intense pink. 1½ft (45cm).

'Bronze Elegance' (Arends, 1956)   Sprays of rose pink over colourful dark foliage. 1ft (30cm).

'Dunkellachs' (Arends, 1952)   Tapering spikes of salmon pink. Glossy dark foliage. 1½ft (45cm).

A. 'Praecox Alba' (Arends, 1952)   Pure-white flowers. Flowering a little earlier than most. 1½ft (45cm).

'Sprite' ('Bloom')   A superlative introduction. Sprays of drooping shell-pink flowers over glossy dark-green leaves. 9in (22.5cm).

'William Buchanan'   Compact glossy bronzed foliage with creamy-white flowers. 6in (15cm).

Cardamine (Order Cruciferae) (Lady's Smock, Cuckoo Flower)

The name is derived from *kardamine*, a diminutive form of *kardamon*, cress, used by Dioscorides. Hardy perennials thriving in a damp shady or sunny situation in most kinds of soil. *C. latifolia* (broad-leaved) has purplish flowers in June. The leaves are large smooth and pinnate. The species is a native of the Pyrenees. *C. pratensis* (meadow) is a native of the British Isles and common in wet meadows. A much smaller plant than *latifolia*. The flowers are usually white or pale-purple whilst the foliage has a cress-like appearance. There is a double form, 'Flora Plena', which is particularly attractive. Both species and the double form are easily grown in moist soil. Propagation is best achieved by dividing the plants after flowering.

Cimicifuga (Order Ranunculaceae) (Bugwort, Bugbane)

The name comes from *cimex*, a bug, and *fugo*, to drive away, indicating the odour that the foliage of some of the plants possesses. Graceful late-summer and autumn-flowering hardy perennials thriving in moist rich soil in light shady borders. Although most grow from 4 to 6ft (1.2–1.8m) they rarely need any sort of support. All are easily propagated by division of the rootstock in the spring.

C. cordifolia   A native of North America. Dark olive green cordate (heart-shaped) foliage with slender spires of light-brown buds that open out to creamy-white flowers during August.
C. racemosa   Light-green triternate dissected foliage with long racemes of white flowers on 4ft (1.2m) stems during July and August.
C. ramosa   A superlative October-flowering species with similar green foliage. The 6ft (2m) arching stems carry pure-white large bottle-brush-like flowers. A group of these is simply irresistible when planted in a rich moist soil in light shade.
C. ramosa 'Atropurpurea'   The purplish stems and foliage of this variety make it quite outstanding – contrasting well with the pure-white flowers. Propagation is by division only, in order to obtain plants identical to the parent. Seed-raised plants may produce some purple-tinted ones but they will not be true.

C. simplex Another autumn-flowering species, not so tall but equally graceful and possibly more suited to the smaller garden. 'White* Pearl' is a selected form from the 1920s while 'Elstead Variety' is superb, with purplish buds opening to pure-white flowers with pink stamens. 4–5ft (1.2–1.5m). The species often flowers into early November, depending on the season. All the late-flowering species make a valuable contribution to damp woodland borders or waterside planting, thus extending the season.

Decodon (Order Lythraceae) (*Nesaea verticillata*) (*Swamp Loosestrife*)

A native of North America, this is an uncommon plant, probably on account of its having rather inconspicuous mauve *Lythrum*-like flowers during the summer. However, it is a useful shrubby plant, growing to 5ft (1.5m) or so, for the banks of the larger water garden where it will give good autumn colour of a rich brilliant crimson. It is easily propagated by cuttings rooted in mud.

Eupatorium (Order Compositae)

Eupatorion is a name used by Dioscorides. Pliny says that it was named after Mithridates Eupator, King of Pontus, who discovered that one of the species had medicinal properties. A large and diverse family of over 400 species, only two of which are considered suitable for inclusion in the bog garden or for waterside planting.

E. cannabinum Hemp agrimony is a handsome native of the British Isles, Europe and Asia. A tall-growing plant with downy lanceolate leaves on reddish erect downy stems and surmounted by tufts of reddish-purple florets. Likes a wet alluvial soil, and, as it grows to 4ft (1.2m) or more and seeds itself freely, it can be used to good effect in a wildlife pool containing other native plants.

E. purpureum (North American Joe-pye-weed or trumpet weed) This plant makes an arresting sight beside the larger water garden in late summer. Large flat heads of purple flowers on 6–10ft (2–3m) smooth purple stems with dark-green pointed leaves in whorls round the stem.

Filipendula (Order Rosaceae) (*Meadowsweet*)

These plants were once known as *Spiraea*. They all require moist-to-wet soil in sun or light shade. In their natural habitat of wet meadows the moisture content is conserved by the natural vegetation, but in the cultivated soil of a garden a mulch of compost or well rotted manure may be necessary to maintain an adequate moisture level. All have feathery plumes and pinnate or peltate foliage. Propagation is by division of the rootstock either in spring or autumn. Mention should be made here of the odd one out. *Filipendula hexapetala* and its double form 'Plena' require ordinary garden soil with no special requirements for moisture content. They are distinguished by the distinctive finely cut feathery foliage and should not be included in any planting scheme in the bog garden.

F. digitata   This may be a doubtful name for a species that grows to 2ft (60cm) or so with pinnate foliage and heads of pale pink flowers in July.

F. palmata (Spiraea camtschatica, S. gigantea)   Various synonyms are attributed to this plant. In fact, I find that the nomenclature of this family is quite misleading, and I have noticed that several other gardening authors are equally confused. The plant I knew as *Spirea camtschatica* is some 6ft (2m) tall with broad palmate foliage with large loose heads of small white flowers. *F. palmata* has, as its name implies, palmately lobed leaves with stout 2–3ft (60–90m) stems bearing large flat heads of rose-crimson flowers. There is also an attractive white form of the preceding called 'Alba'.

F. venusta 'Magnifica' (syn. *rubra, lobata*) (queen of the prairie) A superb North American species and well known for its dark green pinnate foliage on strong 5–6ft (1.5–2m) stems that rarely need staking. The large wide heads of feathery deep-pink flowers are at their best in July.

F. ulmaria   The true meadowsweet, growing in damp or wet meadows, ditches and stream sides. The variety 'Aurea' is an attractive form with pure clear yellow foliage. Planted in shade the leaves tend to be green tinged with yellow. I find it best in moist humus-rich soil in sun. These conditions also thwart the threat of mildew which sometimes attacks the plants if grown on the dry side. If the flower heads form, they should be removed in order to encourage new fresh yellow foliage through to the autumn. The double form of the meadow sweet, *F. u.* 'Flora Plena', is more of a desirable plant than the species, again very suitable for wet humus-rich soil in sun to avoid possible attacks of mildew. *F. u.* 'Rosea' is an uncommon variety with palest pink flowers on 3ft (90cm) stems. *F. u.* 'Variegata' is a sparsely variegated meadowsweet with a blotch of gold on each leaf. It may appeal to devotees of anything variegated but otherwise it is rather poor.

Geum rivale (Order Rosacea) (Water Avens)

A native British plant found growing in shady areas by streams mainly in the north and north-west of England. Suitable therefore for inclusion in the damp areas of a wildlife pond. It will form dense clumps of attractive foliage with slender branching stems bearing nodding sprays of pinkish-red flowers. A selected form of the wild water avens is *G. r.* 'Leonard's Variety', which has larger rich-coppery-pink flowers, not quite as vigorous as the species though it is well worth growing in the damp border.

Gunnera (Order Haloragidaceae)

The plant was named in honour of J. E. Gunner (1718–1773), a Swedish bishop and botanist. *Gunnera manicata* is the largest of all herbaceous foliage plants growing in Great Britain. It was found in the shady ravines of the Andes, where the enormous rough leaves are often 4–5ft (1.2–1.5m) in width on thick bristly stems some 12ft (3.6m) high, providing sufficient shelter for a pony and its rider from a heavy rainstorm. Yet beside a lake or a large water garden it is unsurpassed. The flower spikes, too, are enormous, bottle-brush-like, with a mass of unopened flowers that turn red as the season progresses. To attain such proportions the plant must have constant moisture at its roots and a very rich soil.

Top dress each spring with well rotted manure or compost. The first frosts of the winter will destroy the beauty of the leaves. This is the time to bend them over and place them uppermost over the crowns. In normal winters this should suffice, but in severe winters, as an added precaution, a covering of straw or bracken will be necessary. In the spring the new growths will emerge, pushing through the old leaves and straw, which will act as an excellent mulch. Propagation is by division of the crowns in the spring just as growth commences. This is also the best time for planting. Autumn planting is too risky: the crowns will not become sufficiently well established to withstand the winter. Some success can be achieved from seed sown in heat in the spring but birds have an uncanny way of distributing seed in the most unlikely spots around the nursery or garden. I have found the occasional seedling in pots of alpines some 30–40 yards (30–40m) away. *G. scabra* is similar except that the leaves remain funnel-shaped and are not so flat and the seed heads have a pubescent touch to them. There is also a diminutive species, *G. magellanica*, a real lilliputian by comparison, growing no higher than 2–3in (5–7.5cm). Suitable for carpeting damp shady areas.

Hemerocallis (Order Liliacea) (Day Lily)

The name was used by Theophrastus: *hemero* means a day and *kallos* beauty – an allusion to the short-lived splendour of the individual flower.

These hardy herbaceous plants are long-lived and unsurpassed for waterside planting. Indeed, they will thrive in any herbaceous border that is in full sun and with a soil that is in good heart, though they will not tolerate waterlogged conditions. The leaves are generally long and narrow, some are grass-like and all are radial. The individual flowers are ephemeral but are produced in abundance over a long period. Easily increased by division at almost any time, though spring and autumn are best.

Of the hundreds of varieties available today, due to the hybridization work carried out first in this country and more recently in America, I can only highlight some personal favourites. It is a little disconcerting that the species are not better known or more readily available, as these have given rise to the many hybrids. In the species are to be found some delightful yellows. The flowers are small but most are richly scented with rushy foliage. *H. dumortieri* opens the season in May with deep-yellow flowers from brown buds. Occasionally the flowers are formed nestling within the dense grassy foliage. More often, though, the stems grow to 2ft (60cm). This is followed by *H. middendorfiana*, whose flowers are of a warm orange-yellow with broader foliage forming a dense clump. Both species are natives of Siberia and Japan. *H. flava* (*H. lilio-asphodelus*) has clear-yellow flowers in midsummer and is the only European species found mainly in eastern Europe. It has been grown in Britain since the sixteenth century. A really beautiful plant with a delightful fragrance. *H. fulva* is another old plant native to Japan. Vigorous and free-flowering with broad foliage. The large lily-shaped flowers which are on strong 3ft (1m) stems are of a soft red-brick colour. There is a double variety called 'Kwanso Flora-Plena' which has reddish-orange flowers. It is vigorous and free-flowering and capable of forming great clumps. *H. Fulva* 'Kwanso Variegata' is a variegated form which has spectacular foliage broadly striped with white. It is less vigorous and particularly uncommon. *H. multiflora* is the last species to flower, usually in August and September. It has stems with branching heads, each with small flowers of pale orange-yellow.

There are other species but they are rarely seen except in a botanic garden.

The early hybridists George Yeld and Amos Perry raised many beautiful varieties, mainly of the orange and amber shades, such as 'Gold Dust' (1906), 'Apricot' (1913), 'Orangeman' (1906) and 'Margaret Perry' (1925). There were others but sadly they may no longer be in cultivation. But these were the forerunners of the multitude of varieties that we have today. Most of these, however, have been raised since the war in the United States. I have always had a preference for the yellow and orange shades such as 'Hyperion' (clear yellow) and 'Whichford' (primrose yellow). Both of these are large-flowered and scented. 'Doubloon' is pure gold. I do not consider mauve and purple as day-lily colours, nor do I like those with ruffled petals. Two excellent reds are 'Stafford' and 'Alan', and 'Pink Damask' is probably the best pink. 'Golden Chimes' is first-rate. This has small yellow flowers on branched stems in June and July. This variety is probably descended from *H. multiflora* as it is somewhat similar.

Hosta (Order Liliacea) (*Funkia*)

The genus *Hosta* is of east Asiatic origin and this is as far as I intend to go on any of the technical details, since much has been written by several authorities in recent years, giving much detailed information on the history, the cultivation and the many varieties that are now available. All agree that these are beautiful garden plants, slowly forming clumps of superb foliage with spikes of elegant lily-like flowers, usually mauve, violet or white. They are probably seen at their best beside water or in damp borders in light shade, where the best leaves are produced from a soil that is humus-rich but well drained (they will not tolerate waterlogged conditions).

Of the many varieties now available – including the new introductions from the United States and those raised by the late Eric Smith, who has probably done more than anyone else in Britain in recent years in hybridizing and making these plants so popular (particularly his numerous blue-leaved varieties such as 'Buckshaw Blue', 'Halcyon', 'Tardiana' and 'Blue Moon') – I shall highlight some personal favourites which I have grown with much pleasure during the past thirty years. At long last the names of many, hitherto in a state of confusion, are now being rectified in accordance with the authorities accepted in Britain (Brickell, Hylander, Thomas and others). Nevertheless, I give all the known synonyms in brackets if they are still widely used.

I particularly like *H. sieboldiana* 'Elegans', whose large leaves are blue-grey and more rounded and distinctly furrowed than *H. sieboldiana*. Spikes of palest blue or white flowers protrude just above the foliage. The clone that I have grown for many years came from the old Sunningdale Nurseries during the 1960s, when Graham Thomas was there. 'Frances Williams' ('Gold Edge') originally from Bristol Nurseries, Connecticut, USA, is similar in size and texture but with a broad yellow edge. The name 'Thomas Hogg' appears to cover several white-edged clones in British gardens. The one I have grown for many years under this name is vigorous with pointed green leaves broadly edged with white. *H. crispula*, however, is quite distinct. The leaves are much larger and longer. They are deep green and undulate and are broadly edged with white. *H. fortunei* 'Albo-picta' (*H.f.* 'Picta' *H.f.* 'Aureo-maculata') is sometimes known as the Chelsea hosta on account of the superb display it makes in the outside garden. The spring foliage is lemon-yellow edged with green. This is a striking and popular plant but turns entirely green by midsummer. *H. fortunei* 'Aurea' is an older variety with leaves entirely lemon-yellow in spring gradually fading to green by summer. *H. fortunei* 'Obscura-marginata', also known as 'Yellow Edge', has a distinctive creamy yellow band that surrounds the broad grey-green foliage, and this colouring lasts right through the summer. *H. undulata* ('Undulata medio-variegata') is a smaller and more compact plant than the *fortunei* variety, with clumps of bright-green wavy-edged leaves. The central variegations are creamy white and splashed pale green. Spikes of lavender flowers are produced from June to July. *H. ventricosa* has heart-shaped foliage of shiny deep green. This hosta has the best flowers of all, large and bell-shaped, of a deep purple colour. *H. ventricosa* 'Variegata' is even more outstanding, with the foliage broadly edged with creamy-yellow. *H. plantaginea* 'Grandiflora', an old variety used to great effect by Gertrude Jekyll, forms large clumps of shiny yellow-green foliage with huge scented pure-white flowers in late summer through to the autumn. It needs a sheltered warm site with moisture to flower well. It is not so successful if grown in the midlands and the north. *H. albo-marginata alba* (*H. minor alba*) has neat mounds of small, narrow green leaves with 18in (45cm) spikes of white flowers in late summer – a useful plant for the smaller border.

That completes my short list of favourites. Obviously there are more but these represent a fair cross-section of the diversity of such architecturally fine plants. To keep the foliage unblemished from slugs and snail damage you will need to be liberal with slug pellets.

Hostas are easily propagated by division in spring or autumn, although I find that August is a good time, particularly if the foliage of some of the variegated forms has become a little worn. Lift the clumps and divide the crowns in the normal way, reduce the foliage and trim back the roots, replant, water well in and in a few weeks new foliage will appear which will look good through to the autumn. Hastening propagating material from a particularly rare or slow-growing hosta can be achieved by cauterizing a single crown in the spring before growth starts. It is not a job for the faint-hearted! Dust the wounded sides with sulphur to prevent fungal diseases setting in, then plant in a well prepared bed with added grit or, alternatively, pot up the dissected crowns in a potting compost with added grit.

Inula magnifica (Order Compositae)

This is a robust plant requiring a lot of space. Very suitable for the wilder areas of the bog garden or at the water's side, where it can be a majestic sight with its towering 6ft-tall (2m) stems topped with 6in (15cm) deep-yellow shaggy flower heads in July and August. It is a native of the Caucasus.

Iris (Order Iridaceae)

This large and diverse genus contains species and their varieties that thrive in hot, dry situations through to permanently damp and wet conditions, and some submerged in shallow water. There are three reasonably distinct groups. *I. kaempferi, I. laevigata* (dealt with in Chaper 5) and *I. sibirica*. The most important one in this section is undoubtably *Iris kaempferi* (called by some botanists *I. ensata* because of its sword-shaped leaves). These are the Japanese or clematis-flowered irises of the paddy fields, where they will tolerate being submerged in shallow water for short periods only during the summer months. Far better to grow them in a rich, moisture-retentive lime-free soil in full sun. No bog garden can be complete without these majestic irises, but, to give them the justice they deserve, plant them in groups in a bed to themselves or in large drifts at the lake side with no neighbouring plant flowering in competition. To provide continuity of colour, however, group the *I. kaempferi* with say *Trollius* for the spring display (these should be over by June when the *I. kaempferi* are in bloom) and with perennial lobelias for late summer flowering. In the very early 1900s the colour range was exceedingly mixed in Japan – from deep blue to

Iris kaempferi.

pink and white, mottled, striped and self colours. Since then, Japanese nurseries as well as nurserymen in this country and in America have been hybridizing *I. kaempferi* and have given clonal names to the most distinct and outstanding. Some nurseries now list a dozen or more. You will need to seek them out since most are offered as mixed hybrids. There is also a variegated form with purple flowers.

The third group of waterside irises, the *sibirica* varieties, are less demanding of moisture than the *I. kaempferi*. Nevertheless, they do require a good moisture-retentive soil, particularly during the summer.

I. chrysographes A Chinese species with deep purple-red flowers and grassy foliage. There are also some very worthwhile forms with very dark velvety purple flowers such as 'Black Knight' and 'Black Strain'. 'Margot Holmes' (Perry, 1927) is a hybrid with *I. douglasiana*. This has purple-crimson flowers lined with gold towards the throat. Both grow to 1½–2ft (45–60cm) and flower in June.

I. monnieri 'Monspur' (*monnieri* × *spuria*) and *I. ochroleuca* (*I. orientalis*) These are similar in growth and habit, all having sword-shaped blue-grey foliage between 3 and 5ft (90–150cm) tall and thriving in ordinary garden soil that is not too dry. They look particularly dramatic beside water, provided that their roots are kept away from permanently boggy conditions. 'Monspur' has large pale-blue flowers. Two notable old varieties are 'Cambridge Blue' (Barr, 1924) and 'Dorothy Foster', which is a soft mauve (Foster 1899). *I. ochroleuca* is white with yellow falls. *I. spuria* can be a variable Spanish species with bold sword-shaped foliage. The flowers are pale blue deepening to soft purple. In more recent years a number of hybrids have been raised to include a wide range of colours.

I. kaempferi is easily raised from seed if sown as soon as ripe or in the following spring. Dividing the clumps is best done in early autumn before the growth has completely died down. The other irises can be divided after flowering.

I. sibirica The specific name could be a little misleading since this *Iris* is a native of central and eastern Europe, though it does stretch to western Siberia and is naturally blue. This soundly perennial group has been far too long the 'forgotten' iris of the genus, which need not have been since their cultural demands are few, they are not invasive, seldom need dividing and look superb in a rich, moist soil in full sun, where they will produce attractive grass-like foliage and an abundance of blue flowers in varying shades on 3ft (90cm) stems. They will also grow well in ordinary soil in the herbaceous border. *I.s.* 'Perry's Blue' (old china blue), 'Emperor' (deep-violet blue) and 'Caesar' (violet-purple) are some of the older pre-war varieties which are still worthy of cultivation. However, during the last few years a number of interesting hybrids have been bred in Britain and elswhere. Some notable ones include 'Anniversary' (M. Brummett, 1965), pure-white flushed yellow at the throat; 'Limeheart' (M. Brummett, 1968), white with greenish veins; and an even newer British cultivar, 'Clee Hills' (J. Hewitt, 1979), with violet-blue flowers. As with all the newer hybrids, the petals are wide and tend to stand out horizontally rather than falling loosely like the older cultivars. One of the most striking of the new cultivars is 'Flight of Butterflies' (J. Witt, 1979), a little shorter than most at 2½ft (75cm). The flowers are small and exceedingly dainty, dark blue with paler falls heavily veined with purple. With all *siberica* irises the seed heads are most attractive in the autumn and winter. They will hold their form or they can be picked for indoor winter decorations.

I. versicolor A native of North America, the form 'Kermesina' has particularly attractive flowers of a rich ruby-red. Free-flowering, this iris enjoys a damp to wet soil in sun. There is a hybrid (*I. versicolor* × *I. virginica*) of recent years known as 'Gerald Darby' where young spring foliage is unmistakably deep purple and the flowers are blue, veined purple. Both grow to 2ft (60cm). As with all irises flowering begins in June and extends into July.

Kirengeshoma palmata (Order Saxifragaceae)

A very beautiful yet still comparatively rare herbaceous perennial from Japan. Although generally considered a woodlander, enjoying a humus-rich lime-free soil in light shade, it does prefer it to be moisture-retentive and so is adaptable in the higher reaches of the bog garden. The purplish 3–4ft (90–120cm) arching stems give rise to sprays of strange thick wax-like yellow buds which open to small shuttlecock flowers in early autumn. The seed germinates readily if sown in the spring. The main problem, however, is ensuring that the seed pods ripen before the onset of winter as so often they just drop off. Suitably warm late-summer and early-autumn weather and well-grown established clumps are essential for the seed to ripen. Dividing the clumps in spring is, of course, a guaranteed method. Late spring frosts can damage the youngest emerging growth and so can slugs and snails, but otherwise it is perfectly hardy.

Leucojum aestivum (Order Liliaceae) (Summer Snowflake or Loddon Lily)

Leucoion, the Greek name used by Theophrastus from *leukos*, white, and *ion*, violet refers to the colour and fragrance of the flowers. A European species, including Great Britain and said to be found growing on the banks of the River Loddon and elsewhere. 'Gravetye Giant' is a selection of *L. aestivum* made by that great English gardener William Robinson. This has extra-large daffodil-like leaves with large drooping clusters of from four to six flowers on stems 2–3ft (60–90cm) tall. A very desirable plant for moist or very moist areas in the bog garden in sun or in light shade.

Ligularia (Order Compositae) (Senecio)

The plants of this genus belong to the ragwort family but none are invasive and all are very distinct. All species and their varieties rate as excellent bog-garden plants, requiring an abundant amount of moisture during the growing season. They are also prone to slug and snail damage in spring and summer.

L. clivorum (dentata) 'Desdemona'   A most handsome plant with large purplish dentate foliage on 3–4ft (90–120cm) stalks. The rich orange-yellow rayed flowers on strong branched stems protrude well above the foliage in July and August, providing a striking combination of colour. Self-sown seedlings will occur, with the possibility of some with even deeper coloured leaves. *L. clivorum* has plain green leaves and is more robust. Ideal for mass planting by the waterside.
'Gregynog Gold'   Raised in 1950 from a cross (*L. dentata* × *L. veitchiana*), this has similar-coloured flowers to *clivorum* but they are arranged in crowded cone-shaped spikes some 5ft (1.5m) tall. *L.* × *hessei* (*L. dentata* × *L. veitchiana* × *L. wilsoniana*) is very similar. Both these hybrids have large dentate green foliage.
L. hodgsoni   This is less well known and less tall, but an attractive species with rounded saw-edged leaves of a purplish hue. Although growing to only about 2ft (60cm), it has similar-coloured flowers on stout stems. A compact plant, so more suited to the smaller garden.
L. japonica and *L.* × *palmatiloba*   The second is a hybrid between *dentata* and *japonica*. These two are similar, both having palmate deeply cut leaves and orange flowers in clusters on strong 5ft

(1.5m) stems in August and September. Of the two × *palmatiloba* may be slightly superior.

L. macrophylla The plant that I grow came from Bressingham Gardens in England and differs slightly from the one Graham Thomas describes in his book *Perennial Garden Plants*. The one from Bressingham Garden has dark-green lanceolate leaves with strong 5ft (1.5m) stems carrying crowded heads of yellow flowers.

(a)

(b)

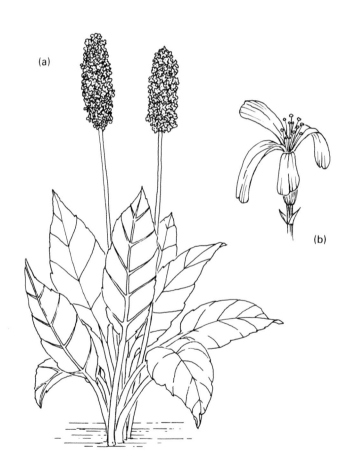

Ligularia macrophylla *showing habit* (a) *and detached flower head* (b).

L. przewalskii (Senecio przewalskii) 'The Rocket' is an especially good form of the species, having heart-shaped jagged-edged leaves on near-black stems. The 4–5ft (1.2–1.5m) flower stems are also almost black and carry tapering spires of starry yellow flowers in July and August. It needs a rich, very moist but not waterlogged soil to do well.

L. veitchiana   A robust Chinese species with large circular green leaves. The stiff 5ft (1.5m) spikes from the base bear yellow daisy-like flowers on branched panicles in late summer.

All the *Ligularia* species and hybrids can be divided in the autumn or spring.

Lilium (Order Liliaceae)

There is a small group of *Lilium* species from this vast and varied genus which are adapted for growing in a soil with a higher moisture content than would suit the other members, though they still require good drainage in sun or light shade. Those listed are from America and are known collectively as American swamp lilies.

L. canadensis   A native of the eastern United States and Canada. The graceful flowers vary from yellow to red with an abundance of purplish-brown spots. It grows from 2 to 4ft (60–120cm) in open moist borders and is in flower in June and July.

L. carolinianum   This can be regarded as a smaller edition of *L. superbum* with its fragrant orange flowers heavily spotted with purple. Although this lily is sometimes called southern swamp lily, like most other moisture-loving lilies it will not survive if planted in a saturated bog where the bulbs would rot.

L. pardalinum   Sometimes called the western tiger lily. The stems up to 6ft (2m) carry clusters of orange-yellow flowers spotted half-way and blending into a bronze shade of red at the tips. They should be planted 8in (20cm) deep.

L. superbum   Also called the American Turk's cap and swamp lily. Possibly the most beautiful and showy of all the native North American species. This lily is the only one that will succeed in very moist lime-free soil – even boggy conditions – in light shade. Very tall, often 6–8ft (2–2.6m), with typical stems carrying up to thirty handsome flowers of crimson-orange, heavily spotted. Care is necessary to avoid damage when planting the bulbs, which resemble old fashioned dumb-bells used for exercising. Plant 8in (20cm) deep in the autumn. It flowers during July and August.

Lobelia (Order Campanulaceae)

Named in honour of Matthies de L'Obel (1538–1616), a botanist and physician to James I, this is a large genus comprising 200 or so varied species of hardy, half-hardy, annual or perennial plants. It is often hard to understand why the well-known annual *Lobelia* used so extensively as a bedding plant should be of the same family as the perennial that we know as *Lobelia cardinalis* or *L. fulgens*, but on closer examination it will be noticed that the flowers of both are very similar. With the tall herbaceous *Lobelia*, the flowers are tubular with the tube cleft on the upper side, thickened or ventricose at the base. The lower lip of the flower is three-forked and pendulous while the two segments of the upper lip are linear-lanceolate. The flower stem from compact rosettes grows from 2 to 4ft (60–120cm), with the leaves alternate and usually sessile. These tall-growing herbaceous lobelias are among the most distinctive and stately plants in the water garden and for late summer and early autumn colour they are unrivalled. They are native of North America and Mexico, thriving best in a rich, very damp soil that does not dry out during the summer. Although almost hardy, they do not appreciate unpredictable British winters of alternating cold and mild spells. It is best to try to stabilize winter conditions by a covering of straw or ashes some 2–3in (5–7.5cm) thick. Incorporate in this a quantity of slug bait to prevent the almost certain slug damage that occurs in the early spring. This should satisfy their chief demands through this somewhat difficult period. Alternatively, the clump can be lifted in November and placed in a cold frame until the spring – but ventilate whenever possible.

L. cardinalis (cardinal flower)   The true plant is now quite rare in gardens. It was introduced from North America in 1626. From bright green leafy rosettes grow 3–4ft (90–120cm) spikes with the brightest scarlet flowers. They require a rich soil that is assured of an ample supply of moisture during the summer. Although *L. cardinalis* is subject to severe winter weather in its native habitat it is protected by the natural vegetation. In Britain, however, where the plants are grown in cultured gardens, they will need protection. Nevertheless, plants sometimes do die out as a result of winter conditions or slug damage. Therefore, in order to keep up the stock, seed should be saved and sown in the early spring under glass, where it will readily germinate. Prick out the seedlings in the usual manner. When sufficiently large, they can then be planted out into well prepared borders.

(a)

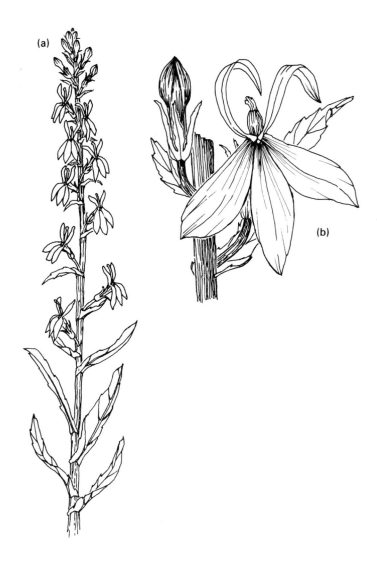

(b)

Flowering stem of Lobelia cardinals (a), *and* Lobelia speciosa
*'Queen Victoria' showing detached portion of stem with bud and fully
opened flower* (b).

L. fulgens   This handsome half-hardy perennial was introduced from Mexico in 1809. The flowers, which are larger than *L. cardinalis*, are a rich, dazzling scarlet. The long, narrow leaves on the round stems grow to about 2ft (60cm) and are a deep purple-red and have a downy appearance. Some fine hybrids have been raised from this or from crosses between *L. cardinalis* and *L. syphilitica* and *L. fulgens* and are offered as *L. fulgens hybrida*. Of the older hybrids that have stood the test of time 'Queen Victoria' and 'Bees' Flame' are outstanding. Both have large dazzling scarlet flowers, the former being taller at 4–5ft (120–150cm). They thrive best in a rich peaty soil in a sheltered but sunny border that has an abundant amount of moisture. Contrary to popular belief, submerged in a garden pool it will not live for more than a few weeks before the plant begins to deteriorate. Being less hardy than *L. cardinalis*, protection will be necessary. Other varieties that were raised long ago include 'Huntsman', with large bright scarlet flowers. 'Mrs Humbert' may now be something of a rarity; it seems that it is listed by only one or two nurseries now. Raised in the early part of this century, it has pure-rose-pink flowers and is dwarf in comparison with other hybrids. 'Russian Princess' also has pink flowers, contrasting well with the dark-purple-red downy foliage. 'Jack McMasters', a hybrid of more recent years, has lavender-purple flowers on 3ft (90cm) stems over green rosettes.

More recently, crosses have been made at the Research Institute of Agriculture in Ottawa, Canada. The aim was to produce vigorous plants with large flowers which should prove hardier than the older hybrids. The species used were *L. syphilitica*, *L. cardinalis* and the cultivars 'Queen Victoria' and 'Illumination'. It has been a complex process and the hybrids that have been produced are now named *Lobelia* × *speciosa* 'Sweet'. Listed here are some of the hybrids that were assessed and given clonal names at the Royal Horticultural Society garden at Wisley. They are now becoming more widely available.

'Brightness' has bright-red flowers with pale-green foliage. 'Dark Crusader' has dark velvety-red flowers with purplish-green foliage, but is of weak growth. 'Will Scarlett' is bright red with bronze green foliage. All grow to about 3ft (90cm) and require a rich, damp soil in full sun yet in a sheltered position away from strong winds. Overwatering is never a problem with lobelias, but never plunge them into a garden pool. For sheer brilliance and robustness none can match the original clone of *L. speciosa*, 'Queen Victoria', when grown in a humus-rich wet soil in full sun.

L. × gerardii   This is a hybrid raised by Chabanne and Goujou and is the result of crossing *L. cardinalis* with *L. syphilitica*, producing a more robust plant with stronger stems than either of the species. This hybrid was named after Monsieur Gérard, who was director of the botanical park of Tête d'Or where the hybridization work was carried out towards the end of the last century. *Lobelia gerardii* is a vigorous hybrid and fully perennial, sending up strong stems 3–4ft (90–120cm) tall from green rosettes, with violet-purplish flowers. From this cross, a number of excellent hybrids have arisen. *L. × gerardii vedrariensis* is first-rate. The metallic green rosettes carry strong stems 3–4ft (90–120cm) high bearing violet-purple flowers. 'Tania' a similar hybrid but with rich crimson-purple flowers, while 'Rosenkavalier' is starry pink. Groups of lobelias planted near water so that the colour is reflected present an arresting sight during the summer.

L. syphilitica   A perennial species and a native of north-eastern America but known in Britain since 1665. It is more winter-hardy than most and a parent of many named hybrids. It is not so demanding of summer moisture but does need more frequent dividing and replanting in fresh soil. This is best done in the spring. Rosettes of leafy green leaves with 2ft (60cm) stems that carry clear-blue flowers.

Propagation

There are three methods of increasing stock. The species are easily raised from seed sown in spring under glass or by division of the rosettes during March. Division can also be used to increase the stock of the hybrids. About mid-March, remove any winter covering and lift the established clump. Remove the surplus soil and divide, with care, the clumps into single shoots, ensuring that each has some roots. It may be necessary to use a sharp knife to aid division. Pot singly into 3–4in pots (7–9cm), using a standard potting compost. Water well in and place the pots in a cold frame or greenhouse until established. This should be in May, after the danger of spring frosts is over. Then plant out into a well prepared border and water well in. If larger quantities are required of the hybrids, cuttings may be taken in late July. For leaf-bud cuttings, select a strong stem that is not too woody, cut to within 6in (15cm) of the base, and remove flowers and terminal shoots. Internodal cuttings are more successful if the cutting is made so that a node comes flush with the soil level in the pot or tray. Insert the cuttings in a 50/50 peat/grit or sharp sand rooting compost. Water well in and cover with polythene and place in a greenhouse. Shade from hot sun if necessary. When rooting takes place, which should be within 3–4 weeks, pot into 3in (7cm) pots, water well in and overwinter in a frost-free greenhouse, but avoid overhead watering during the winter and early spring to prevent crown rot occurring. Plant out into well prepared borders the following May.

Lychnis flos-cuculi (Order Caryophyllaceae) (Ragged Robin)

A well-known plant occurring in marshes, wet meadows and fens in Great Britain and Europe. Generally speaking, this plant would not normally be included as a plant for the garden, but, with conservation and the creating wildlife pools and bogs in cultivated gardens uppermost in the public's mind, I consider it a desirable addition.

It has few narrow leaves but numerous dainty pink flowers divided into four linear segments. It grows to a height of 1–2ft (30–60cm) and is summer-flowering.

Lysichiton (Order Araceae)

The name comes from the Latin *lysis*, loosening, and *chiton*, a cloak – the spathe is cast off after flowering. The genus comprises just two robust species of marsh plants from eastern Asia and North America. The aroid-like flowers emerge before the foliage in April, followed by enormous, almost sessile, dark-green leaves, similar to paddles. Once established, both species will produce seed in abundance which germinates readily in saturated peaty or muddy ditches or where the glutinous seedpods drop. Propagation can also be effected by division of the rootstock but in my opinion this is not a worthwhile proposition; neither is it a satisfactory method. The name 'skunk cabbage' that is sometimes applied to the plant on account of its rather unpleasant odour belongs to the near relative *Symplocarpus foetidus* (see page 106).

L. americanum Pale-yellow erect arum-like flowers often 1ft (30cm) high and in clusters are followed by paddle-like leaves 3ft (90cm) in length. Truly a plant for the larger bog garden or for planting at the water's edge with at most an inch or so of water covering the roots.
L. camtschatense (eastern Asia) Similar in growth to *L. americanum*, but the spathes are white and are smaller and also flowering is a little later. There is a hybrid between the two that produces

creamy-yellow flowers. It is one of those plants that you either instantly like or dislike as grotesque.

Lysimachia (Order Primulaceae) (Loosestrife)

Lusimachion, the old Greek name, comes from *lysis*, 'dissolving', and *mache* 'strife' – an allusion to the supposed soothing qualities of the plant. There are a number of species of this large and diverse family that are well suited for the water garden. *L. ciliata* is a comparatively rare plant that succeeds best in a sunny part of the bog garden. The open heads of clear-yellow flowers standing some 4ft (1.2m) are in character from July to September. *L. nummularia* (creeping Jenny) is a native of Europe and Great Britain. This is a useful plant for growing on damp banks or at the edge of borders in sun or shade. There is a golden leaved form, *aurea*. Both have showy yellow flowers. *L. punctata*, yellow loosestrife, can become an invasive plant in wet areas, so it is best to confine this plant to the wilder parts of the bog garden or to the edge of a larger pool or lake where it can grow without much attention. In confined areas its growth will need curbing. Yellow whorled flowers on 3ft (90cm) stems in summer. *L. vulgaris* is similar in growth and habit.

Lythrum (Order Lythraceae) (Loosestrife)

The name derives from *lythron*, black blood – the colour of the flowers of some species. Very desirable plants for waterside planting, requiring damp to boggy conditions in order to excel. Most are pink through to magenta, grow to 3–4ft (1–1.2m) and flower during the summer. *L. salicaria* is the common purple loosestrife. It has reddish-purple flowers in whorled leafy spikes and grows freely on the margins of streams and lakes in both Britain and Europe. This species has given rise to some fine hybrids. 'Robert' is a good clear pink; 'The Beacon' and 'Firecandle' are deep rosy-red. Both grow to about 3ft (90cm).

L. virgatum   A native of Asia Minor, this species differs from *L. salicaria* in having more branched spikes (*virgatum* means 'twiggy') with purple flowers. Some fine hybrids include 'The Rocket', with deep pink flowers, and 'Dropmore Purple', rosy-purple. Both grow to 2½ft (75cm). Propagation is best effected from cuttings taken during the summer. Division can be difficult from the woody rootstock.

Monarda (Order Labiateae)

The name comes from Nicoles Monarda, or Monardes (1493–1588), a physician and botanist of Seville. *M. didyma* and its varieties need moisture. They are natives of North America and are known as bee balm and Oswego tea, on account of the leaves being used for making tea in Oswego. Infused in boiling water the leaves make a refreshing drink. The leaves are rough and scented on strong squre stems. The flowers are in close heads or whorls. An easily grown plant for a damp border in full sun. Propagation is by dividing the mat-like root system in the autumn. Some useful cultivars include the well-known 'Cambridge Scarlet'. Another old variety is 'Croftway Pink'. 'Blue Stocking' and 'Prairie Night' are both violet-purple. All grow to about 3ft (90cm).

Orchis (Order Orchidaceae) (Dactylorhiza)

Some of the species of this genera of hardy terrestrial orchids are now listed under *Dactylorhiza*. The species described here were formerly classified under *Orchis*, but are now considered members of the *Dactylorhiza* family. Marsh orchis, *Dactylorhiza latifolia*, is frequently found in basic marshes and bogs of the British Isles but is offered by a few nurseries as 'nursery-grown' tubers. Plant these 3in (7.5cm) deep in a rich soil in sun or light shade in the bog garden. The closely set lilac-purple flower spikes grow to 1½–2ft (45–60cm) in June. *Dactylorhiza fuchsii* is another British native found growing in marshes on basic soils. The leaves are often spotted and flowers are lilac to pinkish-purple. *Dactylorhiza majalis* is found growing in water meadows and fens mainly in southern England. Grown in humus-rich moist soil, the small hand-like tubers will increase freely, but transplanting and propagation of the tubers should be carried out only in the autumn months when the growth of the tubers will have fully matured.

Peltiphyllum peltata (Order Saxifragaceae) (Umbrella Plant)

The name comes from *peltata*, a shield, and *phyllon*, a leaf, from the form of the leaves. A native of California but a perfectly hardy perennial for the waterside requiring a rich soil of boggy conditions. The circular indentate leaves will reach 3–4ft (90–120cm) on single stems by midsummer, and later assume colourful autumn tints. The large umbels of pink flowers are produced on naked 2ft (60cm) stems during April and May, before the foliage. The creeping thick stoloniferous rootstock is useful for protecting the banks of streams and sloping areas around natural pools from erosion.

Petasites (Order Compositae)

The Greek name was used by Dioscorides and comes from *petasos*, an umbrella, on account of the size of the leaves. Vigorous and rampant plants suited only for the wild damp woodland areas, although *P. fragrans* (winter heliotrope) has fragränt flat heads, flowering in February and March, before the huge circular leaves mature in late spring or summer.

Polygonum (Order Polygonaceae) (Knotweeds)

The name comes from *polys*, many, and *gonu*, a knee-joint – reference to the numerous joints of the stem. Many knotweeds are not worthy of garden cultivation on account of their vigorous and sometimes uncontrollable growth. A few, though, are excellent for the damp border.

P. bistorta 'Superbum' This variety has clumps of long leathery leaves with stems of pink poker-like flower spikes in spring and early summer.
P. milletii This needs a moist bed in sun to achieve its real value. It has bright-red flowers on spikes only 1ft (30cm) high from clumps of dark-green narrow foliage. Summer-flowering and only slowly increasing in size each season.

Primula (Order Primulaceae)

It would be hard to imagine a bog garden or a situation at the water's edge of a natural stream without some of these most desirable perennials. From the most robust forms of candelabra primulas to more dainty *P. involucrata*, the range of colour and diversity is such that there are primulas in character from the very early spring through the summer until well into August, which proves without doubt that these plants are indispensable.

Primulas are deep-rooted plants and will flourish in a rich, moisture-retentive soil in sun or partial shade. For best effect the seeds can be left to fall around the plants, where they will readily germinate and grow to produce informal groups. They prefer a soil

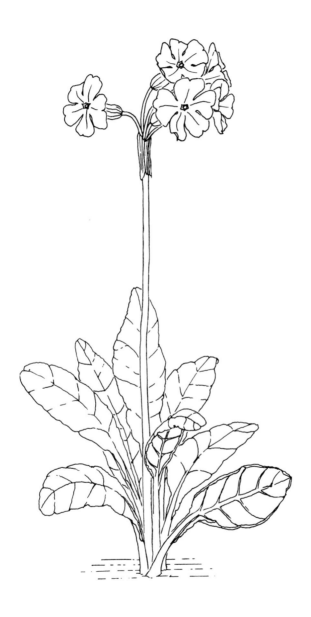

Primula involucrata.

that has a pH value of 5.5–6. If the soil is of a pH of less than 4.5 then a dressing of lime would be beneficial.

All the species and varieties described below require moist conditions, though some will grow in wetter conditions than others. These latter are marked (W).

For simplification I have divided the primulas into five groups. These correspond to five of the thirty sections given in Smith and Forrest (1928) and Smith and Fletcher (1941–1949) (*see* Trehane, *Index Hortensis*), which embrace every primula known in cultivation. (The sections omitted are those not suited for moisture.) The section numbers are given in brackets.

Candelabra (Section 4)

This is one of the most popular groups of waterside primulas. Most are robust growers, producing radial leaves which are usually obovate-spatulate. The flowers are produced in whorls ending in an umbel on stems ranging from 1ft to over 3ft (30–90cm). In a rich, moisture-retentive soil in sun or part shade they are unsurpassed for providing the perfect contrast to the large leaved hostas and rodgersias. They will not do well on an alkaline soil. A neutral soil is preferable.

P. anisodora (1916)   Both leaves and flowers are aniseed-scented (whence the name). Stout stems a foot or so high bearing whorls of dark-crimson flowers with a contrasting clear-yellow eye. As with most candelabra primulas, this species was introduced from western China.

P. aurantiaca (1923)   This is best suited to light shade and is less dependent on moisture than others. It has orange flowers on foot-high (30cm) reddish stems.

P. beesiana (1911)   This species has whorls of rich purple flowers during May and June on 2ft (60cm) stems. It is best grown from seed, as is usual with most primulas. The plants from this may vary in colour from pale mauve to deep carmine. Of vigorous growth, it is fine for the bog garden or for mass planting beside the water's edge.

P. bulleesiana   A hybrid between *beesiana* × *bulleyena* and sometimes known as Asthore hybrids, it produces a wide range of colours from mauve to deep orange.

P. bulleyana (1908)   A beautiful species discovered by George Forrest in the Yunnan. Stout stems bearing whorls of deep-orange-yellow flowers. Needs a damp situation to do well.

P. burmanica (1920)   Reddish-purple flowers with a distinctive yellow eye. The strong 2ft (60cm) stems are free from the white meal that some of the other species have.

P. chungensis (1920) Whorls of orange and red flowers on 1½–2ft (45–60cm) stems during May and June.

P. helodoxa (1912) Another superb species found by Forrest in the Yunnan. Taller than most at 3–4ft (90–120cm). Slender stems with whorls of bright-yellow flowers and pale-green leaves, occasionally crinkled and pointed. Prefers a rich, moist soil but not to the point of saturation or in water. Comes true from seed-raised plants.

P. japonica A robust-growing species bearing stout stems 2–3ft (60–90cm) tall with vermilion-red flowers, very suitable for mass planting in damp woodlands and at the stream side, while some of the selected forms such as 'Miller's Crimson', have deep-magenta flowers. A superlative, easily grown variety, and best in a rich soil with plenty of moisture. This variety will come true from seed-raised plants. 'Postford White' is similar in growth but is white with a yellow eye, useful for brightening up damp shady areas. This will come more or less true from seed if widely separated from other sorts. Occasionally some pinkish flowers may occur but it is a little less reliable than the other *P. japonica* hybrids.

P. 'Inverewe' A superlative clone, flowering in early summer with vivid vermilion-orange flowers in tiered whorls. The buds and stems are heavily farinose. Being sterile, this variety will not set from seed but can be increased by dividing the plants either soon after flowering or in spring, just before growth begins to push through the soil. Requires a rich, moist soil in sun or light shade.

P. poissonii Distinctive from the other candelabra kinds in that this has dark-green glossy rosettes with stems carrying whorls of brilliant magenta flowers in summer. Grows to 1½–2ft (45–60cm).

P. pulverulenta (1905) A graceful species with whorls of rich crimson-purple flowers on 3ft (90cm) stems. Both buds and stems are heavily farinose. Ideal for naturalizing in damp woodland and the stream side. A quite delightful pale-pink *P. pulverulenta* is 'Bartley Strain', which originated from G. H. Dalrymple Bartley Nursery in the New Forest, England during the 1920s.

P. wilsoni Similar to *P. poissonii*, with narrow serrated leaves. Whorls of purple flowers on 3ft (90cm) stems. Best in damp woodland conditions.

Denticulata (Section 9)

P. denticulata (the drumstick primula) is a native of the Himalayas and western China. These easily grown popular perennials will grow in almost any soil that is moisture-retentive but will not tolerate being grown in water. Spring-flowering before the leaves and resistant to frost, they make a delightful contrast planted in association with the *Caltha* (marsh marigold) and *Primula rosea*. The colour ranges from pure white through pale lavender to purple and red shades. There are some selected forms that have been given clonal names. They are easily raised from seed but the named kinds or those with extra-fine colours will need to be propagated from root cuttings to retain their identity.

Farinosae (Section 11)

P. rosea A most desirable early-flowering plant for the bog garden, growing in dense tufts of smooth green leaves often tinged bronze. This primula will thrive with its roots in the running water of a small stream but will do equally well in damp soil. Deep-carmine buds opening to umbels of flowers only a shade lighter on 4–6in (10–15cm) stems. Easily raised from seed.

P. rosea 'Delight' (*Rosea* 'Micia de Geer') (Ruys) An irresistible selection of *P. rosea* with deep-carmine buds and flowers in March and April. This is a much sought-after superior form in both flower and foliage. Propagation is by division only, directly after flowering, as any seed-raised plants will vary in colour and habit.

P. rosea 'Grandiflora' (W) A large-flowered form but the flowers are often paler than *P.* 'Delight'.

P. involucrata Another delightful primula from the Yunnan. Sweetly-scented, white, bell-shaped flowers that dangle on 6–8in (15–20cm) stems from clumps of glossy rounded leaves. Thrives in the bog garden or in a damp corner of the rock garden.

Muscarioides (Section 17)

P. vialli A most unusual primula flowering in June and July and one of the last to appear through the soil, often as late as May. From downy narrow leaves rise stems of deep-purple buds that open to mauve flowers resembling a miniature red-hot poker. Although not strictly a bog garden primula, it does require a rich, moisture-retentive leafy soil to do well. It will also benefit from some shade, where it will reach up to a foot (30cm) in height. It is easily raised from seed and it would be prudent to raise new plants each season as established plants occasionally die out after flowering.

Sikkimensis (Section 26)

This group comprises several true bog plants thriving in very watery conditions where some shade is preferable but not essential. The *P. alpicola* strains are easily cultivated in a rich soil and moisture. All bear umbels of fragrant flowers. *P. alpicola alba* is white, *P. a. luna* is sulphur-yellow, and *P. a. violacea* is variable in colour from mauve to deep violet.

P. florindae (giant Himalayan cowslip) (W)   An outstanding species which when established in a rich wet situation will grow to 3–4ft (1–1.3m) high. Large heart-shaped coarse leaves, with strong stems carrying pendulous umbels of yellow flowers. Ideal for the waterside.

There are a number of excellent selections under various names consisting of coppery and apricot-tinted flowers.

P. ioessa   Often regarded as a dwarf form of *P. sikkimensis*, this grows only to 6in–1ft (15–30cm). The flowers are pale mauve or white.

P. secundiflora   Summer-flowering with wine-red umbels on slender stems 1–1½ft (30–45cm). Fine for damp woodland or bog garden but will not tolerate waterlogged conditions in winter.

P. sikkimensis (Himalayan cowslips) (W)   A very beautiful species with stout stems bearing drooping clusters of pale-yellow fragrant flowers in July. A true bog plant for rich, wet soil and some shade.

Propagation

All the species and their varieties are easily grown from freshly gathered seed unless otherwise stated. Old seed, anything older than nine months, loses much of its viability and seed obtained from sources other than your own, or your friends' gardens is always a doubtful proposition as its age is so often unknown.

Although ideally the seed should be sown soon after gathering, the time that I favour most is easily in the New Year. This is because after sowing the trays or pans of seed compost can be stood outside to stratify and then brought in to a cold frame or greenhouse, where germination will take place usually within six weeks. By June the seedlings can either be pricked off directly into 3in (7cm) pots and stood in a shady area or, if larger quantities are required, they can be lined out into 'nursery' rows, watered well in and kept shaded. By early August these will be ready for either potting up into 3in (7cm) pots or planting out directly into well prepared beds. However, it is often more satisfactory to plant out pot-grown plants during early autumn or spring. Dividing primulas other than the sterile sorts is not worth considering; it is so much easier raising the plants from seed.

Increasing stock of *P. denticulata* other than raising them from seed requires propagation by root cuttings. This method is particularly useful for the named sorts or those with particularly good colours. The easiest way is to thrust a spade under the plant, leaving a good proportion of the roots in the ground. The parent plant can then be replanted in a hole filled with potting compost, where it then grows on. The roots that have been left can then be top-dressed with a similar compost and in due course young plants will appear. After a few weeks they can be lifted and separated and either potted up individually or planted out into permanent quarters.

Ranunculus (Order Ranunculaceae)

The name is the Latin word for a little frog and was used by Pliny for these plants, especially the aquatic species.

R. aconitifolius 'Flora-pleno'   A delightful sixteenth-century plant – the fair maids of France or fair maids of Kent. Palmate deeply toothed dark-green foliage with branching stems that carry pure-white fully double buttons, it is known in gardens as 'White Bachelors' Buttons'. It thrives in a humus-rich soil in full sun or partial shade. Flowering in May and June. Height 2ft (60cm).

Rheum (Order Polygonaceae) (Ornamental Rhubarb)

Sumptuous plants with exotic splendour and well suited to the larger or semi-wild parts of the water garden. They need a deep, rich, moist soil in sun or light shade but do not require so much moisture as gunneras. Propagation is from seed or by division of the crowns in spring, just before growth begins. *R. palmatum* was first found growing wild in 1872–3 by Colonel Prejavalski in the Tangut district of Kansu in the North-West Province of China. This species has palmately lobed apple-green leaves. In May and June it sends up 6–8ft-tall (2–2.5m) shafts with red or white flowers in panicles.

The varieties 'Atrosanguineum' and 'Bowles Variety' are similar clones, both having large deeply cut foliage which is deep-red on the underside and olive-green on the upper side until midsummer, by when most of the brilliant crimson will have become less conspicuous. In June it sends up 5–8ft (1.6–2.5cm) stems with panicles of crimson flowers.

'Ace of Hearts' is a dwarf form more suited to the smaller garden. This is a hybrid raised, from *R. kialence* crossed with a large red-leaved palmatum, resulting in dark heart-shaped leaves beautifully veined and backed with crimson, growing to a height of 2ft (60cm). All species and their varieties are perfectly hardy and do not need any winter protection.

Rodgersia (Order Saxifragaceae)

The genus is named in honour of Admiral John Rodgers (1812–82) of the US Navy, commander of the expedition during which *R. podophylla* was discovered. Aristocratic foliage plants requiring humus-rich wet soil in sun or part shade, suitable for the water's edge. The root system consists of thick scaly rhizomes which give rise to single stems each with large crinkled leaves, alternate peltate or pinnately divided. The numerous flowers are small but in large panicles on 3–5ft (90–150cm) stems. All are natives of China and Japan.

R. aesculifolia Large bronze-tinted horse-chestnut-like leaves. Panicles of creamy-white flowers on 3–4ft (90–120cm) stems.
R. pinnata Pinnately divided foliage. The flowers may be pink or white if grown from seed.
R. pinnata 'Superba' Wrinkled bronze foliage with raspberry pink flowers.
R. podophylla Jaggedly lobed leaves richly burnished to a metallic bronze. The slowly spreading rhizome makes this plant suitable as ground cover in boggy areas. Long-lived and a spectacular species but not so free-flowering as the other species.
R. 'Parasol' A hybrid raised by crossing *R. aesculifolia* and *R. podophylla*, resulting in more rounded leaves. None the less spectacular.
R. sambucifolia Olive-green pinnate elder-leaves with each set separated by a few inches up the stalk. 3ft-tall (90cm) foaming sprays of white flowers.
R. tabularis A distinct species from China with leaves which are circular, slightly indentated and pale-green. They prefer a humus-rich damp soil in light shade where they will reach 3ft (90cm) or more, with each leaf as much as 2ft (60cm) across. An added attraction to this superlative species is the 4–5ft (120–150cm) stems that top the foliage, carrying creamy-white flowers in dense panicles during the summer.

All rodgersias are hardy and can be divided in the autumn or spring.

Salvia (Order Labiatae)

Of the many slightly tender salvias, I have singled out just one which requires more moisture than most – *S. uliginosa* (*uliginosus* means 'of the marshes'). A stately half-hardy perennial, it should be basally hardy in the south but is well worth covering in colder districts. It has 5ft-tall (1.5m) stems with dark-green aromatic foliage with waving wands of pale-blue flowers in late summer. Needs a sheltered sunny spot in damp soil. Easily raised from summer cuttings and overwintered in a frost-free greenhouse.

Senecio (Order Compositae)

The Latin name was used by Pliny and is derived from *senex*, an old man – allusion to the white hair-like downy appearance. Groundsel and ragwort belong to the same family.

S. smithii   A native of the Falkland Islands. From the lush glossy green foliage grow strong 2–3ft (60–90cm) stems bearing branching heads of yellow-centred white daisies which are followed by fluffy white seed heads. A comparatively rare plant requiring a damp to a wet situation in sun or light shade. Propagation is by division in spring.

Symplocarpus (Order Araceae)

A genus of just a single species found growing in the swamps of North America, Asia and Japan.

S. foetidus   This is the true skunk cabbage, growing to about 1ft (30cm) high with 1–2ft-long (30–60cm) cordate leathery leaves. The spathe is spotted and striped purple and yellowish-green and the spadix is globular-shaped, violet and on a short stem. Entirely covered with thickly crowded flowers having a foetid odour similar to that of a skunk. Well suited to growing in wet situations and in bogs. It may be difficult to track down this plant as it is rarely listed in nursery catalogues.

Trollius (Order Ranunculaceae) (Globe Flower)

The name is said to be derived from an old German word, *trol*, a globe. A genus of hardy herbaceous perennials thriving in damp meadows in the temperate regions of the Northern Hemisphere.

T. europaeus, the true globe flower, is also a native of the British Isles, found principally in sub-alpine meadows of Lancashire, North Wales and Scotland. For the bog garden and in almost any moist soil in a sunny situation, *Trollius* species and their numerous varieties are unsurpassed for their display of pale-yellow through to deep incurving orange flowers in spring and early summer. The leaves are alternate, palmately lobed or dissected. The compact crowns arise from a mass of fibrous brown roots. They prefer a loamy soil on the heavy side which is moisture-retentive but not to the point of saturation, particularly during the winter months. Once established, they will flower freely without the need of any support, as most grow to no more than 2–3ft (60–90cm). Division of the numerous hybrids is best made after flowering, August and September being ideal months. Carefully divide the crowns, ensuring that the roots do not dry out during the time they are out of the ground. Reduce the foliage and replant with care; keep the crown near the surface and try not to bury it. Although they require a soil that is in good heart, the roots should not be in contact with manure. It may be necessary to divide every 3–4 years and replant to maintain the vigour of the plant. Seed saved from the species should be sown directly after gathering (though it may be some months before germination takes place). Like all members of the Ranunculaceae family, they are slow to germinate, sometimes taking up to a year.

T. asiaticus This species closely resembles *T. europaeus* but the stems are usually single-flowered and shorter at 1½ft (45cm). The flowers are a darker yellow.

T. acaulis A native of northern India and the Himalayan Mountains. One of the most beautiful dwarf bog plants, growing to only 6in (15cm) in height (*acaulis* means stemless). This diminutive species has bright-yellow flowers up to 2in (5cm) across. It is worthy of a damp or low spot in a rock garden.

T. × cultorum These popular hybrids are derived from *T. europaeus* × *T. asiaticus* and a further cross with *T. chinensis*. A very showy group of these spring flowering plants, producing in the greatest profusion the large incurving globular flowers often 2in (5cm) in diameter on strong 2ft (60cm) stems. The leaves of all this group of hybrids are glabrous and dissected. They are delightful subjects for waterside planting or they can be grown in a herbaceous border provided that the soil does not dry out. A variety with an unusual shade is 'Alabaster', which has pale-primrose or ivory-tinted flowers. Not so robust as the other sorts, but worth the extra trouble for the sake of the distinctive colour. 'Canary Bird' is lemon-yellow and 'Baudirektor Linne' has extra-large golden-yellow flowers and is earlier than most, but the 'Earliest of All', with medium-yellow flowers, is usually the first. 'Fireglobe' ('Feuertroll') is deep-orange-yellow, while 'Orange Princess' is a little paler, 'Goldquelle' golden yellow, 'Byrnes Giant' extra-large lemon-yellow, 'Helios' citron yellow, 'Commander-in-Chief' deep-orange, and 'Empire Day' yellow. And there are others. All flower from May to early June.

T. europaeus (Europe and Britain) (mountain globe flower) A variable plant which, raised from seed, will vary in colour, habit and foliage. *T. europaeus* 'Superbus' is a superlative selection that has lemon-yellow incurved blooms on 2ft (60cm) stems in May.

T. ledebourii (*chinensis*) Quite distinct from the *T.* × *cultorum* hybrids. *T. ledebourii* are taller with less foliage and the flower bowls have prominent orange stamens that stand above the petals. A useful plant because it flowers long after the other hybrids have finished. 'Golden Queen' and 'Imperial Orange' are two hybrids currently available. Both grow to 3ft (1m) and flower during June and July.

T. ranunculoides (*T. patulus*) The orange-yellow flowers are flat and spreading. Height 18in (45cm); mid-summer-flowering.

T. stenopetalus A group of these makes an arresting sight in mid-June. This little-known Chinese species is similar in growth and habit to the other kinds but the flowers are large, open and buttercup-yellow. It grows to about 2ft (60cm) or a little more, depending on moisture.

T. pumilus Another delightful miniature with bright golden flowers only 6in (15cm) high in June.

T. yunnanensis A taller species, native of north-west China. It grows best in a damp sunny spot. It has 2ft-high (60cm) branching stems terminating with golden-yellow single flowers often tipped green at the edges. This flowers a little earlier than the others.

All *Trollius* species and their varieties benefit from a mulch of well rotted compost around the roots in the spring.

ORNAMENTAL GRASSES AND SEDGES

The value of ornamental grasses and sedges is slowly being appreciated by an increasing number of gardeners. There are a number that are suitable for the bog garden and for waterside planting. Some have been mentioned in this book but in no great detail.

Carex elata aurea, Bowles' golden sedge, was until a few years ago comparatively rare in gardens but it is now readily available. It is choice and slow-growing, requiring really boggy conditions to do well. It looks good near water and in full sun, where the colour is at its brightest. In shade, however, the colour is more subdued, often a lime green. *Carex pendula* and *C. pseudacyperus* have graceful drooping spikes and are taller at 4ft (1.2m). *Cyperus longus*, sweet garlingale, is an attractive British native sedge found growing by ponds and in ditches mostly in southern England. It is a useful plant for the larger water garden or for the wildlife pool. The dark-green rough leaves are some 3ft (90cm) tall, with umbels of dark-brown inflorescence. Both are very effective as waterside plants. *Glyceria aquatica* 'Variegata' will grow in shallow water as well as in the bog garden. It is invasive and should be planted with a certain amount of caution. However, its cream, green and pink variegations are attractive during the spring and summer.

There are numerous varieties of *Miscanthus* and all are worthy of inclusion in various parts of the water garden. The tallest and most imposing species is *M. sacchariflorus*, which annually reaches between 8 and 10ft (2.5–3m) in a deep, humus-rich soil that does not dry out during the summer. Its height makes it an ideal windbreak or a leafy backdrop for so many brilliantly coloured perennials. Its annual growth should be cut to ground level every November or before the foliage becomes brittle in order to stop it being blown about the garden. Other varieties of the *Miscanthus* family include *M. sinensis* 'Zebrinus, whose green leaves have transverse golden bands, and *M. sinensis* 'Variegatus', with beautifully variegated white-striped foliage. Both of these are less tall at 4–5ft (1.2–1.5m). There are others in varying degrees of stature and beauty, most growing between 3 and 6ft (90cm–2m). *Spartina pectinata* 'Aureo-marginata' has graceful, arching, gold-edged foliage. It needs a moist spot near water, where it will make an effective clump some 6ft (2m) tall.

All grasses and sedges are best propagated in the spring by lifting the clumps just as growth begins to shoot, carefully dividing, and replanting into a good friable loam with a good supply of moisture at its roots. Pot-grown nursery stock may be safely transplanted during the early autumn as well as in spring.

For further information, see *Ornamental Grasses*, by Roger Grounds, published in 1989 by Christopher Helm in association with the Hardy Plant Society.

8

PLANTING SCHEMES
AND PLANS

This chapter provides examples of planting schemes for preformed pools (fibreglass), using the more flexible materials (butyl), and for natural pools (clay-based). I also include some ideas for the banks of streams and bog gardens. These suggestions are, of course, intended only as a guide, what is important is the suitability of each particular plant, taking into account the vigour and ultimate height and spread in each example shown. This I hope will give gardeners the confidence to select those plants that are right for their particular pond or lake. Some catalogues still offer 'complete collections' for a particular size of pool without defining precisely what the collection of plants consists of. This is a pity because it is rather like buying a pig in a poke: you just do not know what you are going to get. You could end up with easily propagated plants of a rampant nature and totally unsuitable for a garden pond. Likewise with water lilies. So often the white will be either N. × *marliacea* 'Albida' or 'Gladstoniana' – fine for a large pond or lake. N. × *marliacea* 'Carnea', the most common pink, has the same vigour as N. × *marliacea* 'Albida' and neither is suitable for the average-to-small garden pool. It is always best to order plants by name.

Planting in preformed pools leaves you will little scope apart from the one or two water lilies and a few aquatic plants. This is unfortunate as the shelves are only wide enough to accommodate plastic planting baskets, and I have already mentioned my dislike for them. If baskets are to be used, then plant only one variety to each basket.

You will have much more scope planting a pool made from a liner because you can determine the width and the depth of the shelves. This is important if you want to grow aquatics such as *Orontium* which require a deep soil. If you make the shelves wide enough to form an enclosure or pocket by using pieces of rock either protruding out of the water or flat pieces just below the water level and then fill with soil in which to plant, the effect is much more authentic. The pockets can be made to whatever size you wish, depending on the overall size of the pool. Bold groups of some plants are usually more effective.

Planting the margins of a natural running stream can enhance this feature dramatically but first assess the possible rise and fall of the water level over a season. Lengthy periods of flooding, particularly during the winter months, can have a detrimental effect on most waterside plants. Continual flooding (longer than three weeks) would rot such plants as *Astilbe*, *Trollius* and *Rheum*, and most others. In this situation only subjects like *Iris pseudacorus*, *I. laevigata* and *Lysichiton* spp. would survive. For most waterside perennials the water table should be constantly at about 1ft (30cm). Less than this for a few days would not matter, and a wide range of moisture-loving plants will thrive in depths up to 18in (45cm) with good cultivation and an application of a mulch in spring. (The water table is the level at which the subsoil becomes saturated.) The same applies to a bog garden. Excess water lying around the roots of plants, particularly in winter, spells disaster and it is at this time, between November and March, that the water level is most difficult to control.

In the suggestions for bog-garden and streamside garden plants the recommended number of plants per square yard is indicated in brackets after the name of the plant. This, I hope, will give some idea of the spread that they will make after a season or so – with the exception of *Gunnera* and *Rheum*, which are, of course, suited only to large or isolated areas of the water garden.

Plant combinations rarely clash but try to aim at contrasting colours. You may not agree with all my suggestions but they can easily be modified to suit your own particular colour scheme. In the larger water garden, however, you will notice that I favour bold groups of plants of the same variety rather than a lot of different varieties planted together so as to give a patchwork of colour. It should be remembered that in most instances waterside plants growing in a humus-rich soil, with the optimum amount of moisture at their roots throughout the summer, will grow without the interruption of dry spells slowing down their growth. So allowances should be made for what otherwise might be excessive growth. In the listing of the waterside plants and marginal plants I have mentioned particular plants that could colonize an area rapidly. These are best kept to the wilder areas, where they can grow without too much attention or the need to keep their growth limited.

Plan 1

A collection of plants for a pool 5–6ft long, 3–4ft wide and 1½ft deep (2 × 1 × 0.5m).

This selection of aquatics includes a sufficient number of plants, allowing one variety of each to give a complete and attractive effect. The two portions of *Ceratophyllum demersum* are all that is necessary for a pool of this size.

Key to Plan

1 *Nymphaea × laydekeri* 'Lilacea' (rose-pink)
2 *Caltha palustris plena*
3 *Iris laevigata*
4 *Mimulus ringens* } Marginal aquatics plants
5 *Calla palustris*
6 *Scirpus* 'Zebrinus'
   Ceratophyllum demersum (oxygenating plant) (2)
   Hydrocharis morsus-ranae (floating plant)

Plan 2

A collection of plants for a pool 12ft long, 8ft wide and up to 2ft deep (4 × 2.5 × 0.5m).

This selection of aquatics includes a sufficient number of plants to give a complete and attractive effect without becoming rampant and overgrown. Six portions of *Cerataphyllum demersum* are all that is required for a pool of this size.

Key to Plan

1 *Nymphaea* 'Hermine' (pure white)
2 *N.* 'James Brydon' (rose-crimson)
3 *Aponogeton distachyos*
4 *Butomus umbellatus* (2)
5 *Iris pseudacorus* 'Variegatus' (2)
6 *Caltha palustris plena* (2)
7 *Pontederia cordata* (2)
8 *Orontium aquaticum* (1)
9 *Scirpus* 'Zebrinus' (3)

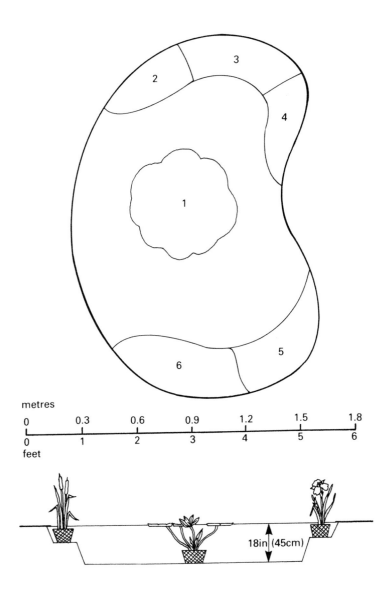

Plan 1.

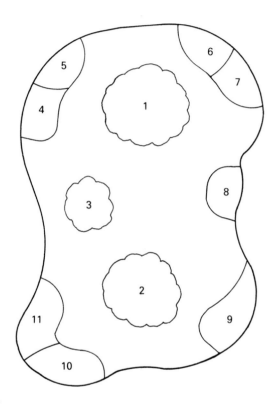

metres

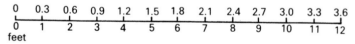

feet

Plan 2.

10 *Iris laevigata* 'Albo-purpurea' (2)
11 *Acorus calamus* 'Variegatus' (2)
    Certophyllum demersum (oxygenating plant) (6)
    Stratiotes aloides (floating plant) (1)

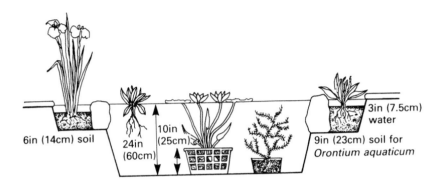

6in (14cm) soil
24in (60cm)
10in (25cm)
3in (7.5cm) water
9in (23cm) soil for *Orontium aquaticum*

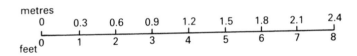

metres
0   0.3   0.6   0.9   1.2   1.5   1.8   2.1   2.4
feet
0   1   2   3   4   5   6   7   8

A cross-section of a pool using a liner where pockets can be made from stone or small pieces of rock on the shelves, replacing the traditional aquatic baskets which are so often inadequate for the larger pool. For planting the water lily, I suggest a basket; 2ft × 1½ft × 10in (60 × 45 × 25cm) (a plastic laundry basket is ideal) is a more accommodating size and the best alternative to soil spread over the base of the pool.

THE LARGE WATER GARDEN

Before starting work on the excavation of any large natural pond (anything over 50ft (15m) in length) that is to be clay-based, thought should be given as to what the subsoil is like and at what depth it will need to be to hold on average 2ft (60cm) of water, allowing, of course, for evaporation. If the subsoil is of a thick yellow clay, what is the best way to deal with it?

So often I have seen the results of these excavations where the clay is nothing but an unworkable heap of material piled up to form an ugly bank encircling the pool. Even when the surrounds have had time to settle, the bank will dry out to a brick-hard impenetrable surface, leaving no scope at all for planting anything. I take the view that any unmanageable excavated clay that increases the height of the natural surrounds by an average of more than 18in (45cm) would look incongruous and is best removed from the site. You will also find it extremely difficult to plant any water lilies in clay or gravel, although this can be overcome by planting in hillocks of soil or by making pockets from weathered bricks and infilling with soil as described in Chapter 2.

Planting water lilies and aquatics in large natural ponds is relatively easy provided that the site remains dry while you construct the various pockets and complete any infilling with soil that is required prior to planting. It is much more difficult, of course, if the pond fills up naturally (over which you have no control) as it is being excavated. In this situation, making pockets, particularly for water lilies, in 2ft (60cm) of water could pose a problem. It would mean wading out with the bricks and buckets of soil.

Another point worth bearing in mind is that for larger ponds of more than ¾ acre (0.3 hectares) in size on farms or in other areas will need advice from your local planning authority. If the pond is to be created in a floodplain or in an existing watercourse, such as a stream or river, then permission will be needed from the National Rivers Authority. Generally speaking, though, anything less than ¾ acre (0.3 hectares) in area will not need planning permission.

Plants for a Large Water and Bog Garden

Key to plan

1	*Rheum palmatum* 'Atrosanguineum'	(1)
2	*Trollius europaeus* 'Superbus'	(4–5)
3	*Iris kaempferi*	(4–5)
4	*Trollius* 'Earliest of All'	(4–5)
5	*Lobelia speciosa* 'Queen Victoria'	(3–4)
6	*Astilbe* 'White Gloria'	(3–4)
7	*Primula pulverulenta*	(4–5)
8	*Caltha polypetala*	(1–2)

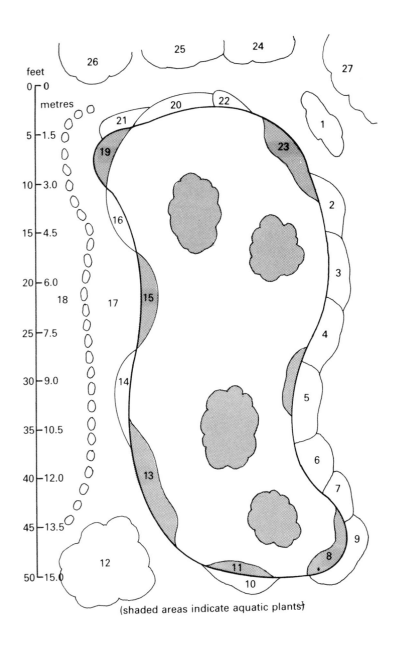

A planting scheme for a large water and bog garden.

(shaded areas indicate aquatic plants)

9	*Hemerocallis* 'Whichford'	(2–3)
10	*Primula bulleyana*	(4–5)
11	*Myosotis palustris* (*scorpiodes*)	(2–3)
12	*Gunnera manicata*	(1)
13	*Scirpus* 'Zebrinus'	(3–4)
14	*Rodgersia aesculifolia*	(2–3)
15	*Iris laevigata*	(3–4)
16	*Astilbe taquettii* 'Superba'	(2–3)
17	*Fritillaria meleagris*	(6–7)
18	*Narcissus bulbocodium*	(6–7)
19	*Iris pseudacorus*	(3–4)
20	*Primula beesiana*	(4–5)
21	*Peltiphyllum peltatum*	(3–4)
22	*Primula sikkimensis*	(4–5)
23	*Butomus umbellatus*	(3–4)
24	*Struthiopteris germanica*	(2–3)
25	*Eupatorium purpureum*	(2–3)
26	*Filipendula camtschatica*	(2–3)
27	*Ligularia hessii*	(2–3)
28	*Nymphaea* 'Gladstoniana'	(1)
29	*Nymphaea* 'Escarboucle'	(1)
30	*Nymphaea* 'Mrs Richmond'	(1)
31	*Aponogeton distachyos*	(3)
32	*Pontederia cordata*	(3–4)

CROSS-SECTION OF A NATURAL POND

The cross-section of a natural pond shows the water depth required (if any) for the aquatics and waterside plants that are planted directly into the pool. It is assumed that the water table remains more or less constant throughout the year, or at most rises a few inches in the winter for not more than a week, otherwise constant waterlogging would rot the roots of some of the perennials, notably astilbes. Similarly, the water should not drop more than a few inches in the summer to the point where some waterside plants would suffer from dryness of the soil. The legend indicates the most suitable positions for a variety of aquatic and waterside plants. Trees that are not overhanging the pond but near enough to provide partial shade to some waterside plants would be beneficial, particularly if the trees are to the north or east of the pond or lake, thus allowing sunlight to the water for at least five hours of the day.

Plants for a Water and Bog Garden

Key to Plan

1	*Trollius* 'Lemon Queen'	(4–5)
2	*Lobelia vedrariensis*	(3–4)
3	*Myosotis palustris*	(2–3)
4	*Orontium aquaticum*	(2–3)
5	*Iris sibirica* 'Perry's Blue'	(3–4)
6	*Trollius* 'Empire Day'	(4–5)
7	*Primula japonica* 'Miller's Crimson'	(4–5)
8	*Rheum tanguticum*	(1)
9	*Pontederia cordata*	(2–3)
10	*Hemerocallis dumorteirii*	(2–3)
11	*Primula florindae*	(3–4)
12	*Primula helodoxa*	(4–5)
13	*Butomus umbellatus*	(2–3)
14	*Caltha palustris plena*	(2–3)
15	*Calla palustris*	(2–3)
16	*Acorus calamus* 'Variegatus'	(2–3)
17	*Astilbe simplicifolia* 'Sprite'	(3–4)
18	*Filipendula palmata*	(2–3)
19	*Iris laevigata* 'Snowdrift'	(2–3)
20	*Ligularia clivorum* 'Desdemona'	(2–3)
21	*Lythrum virgatum* 'The Rocket'	(2–3)
22	*Nymphaea* 'Amabilis'	
23	*Nymphaea* 'James Brydon'	
24	*Astilbe simplicifolia* 'Bronze Elegance'	(4–5)
25	*Astilbe* 'Rhineland'	(3–4)

You will notice that I have recommended the minimum number of plants on the plans, thus allowing for growth to fill the allotted space. I also recommend that just one lily of each variety is planted to allow for ultimate spread and to ensure that at least half to two-thirds of the surface of the water is clear of foliage.

THE STREAM GARDEN

The plants that I have selected for planting in the stream garden will provide colour from the early spring right through to the autumn and winter, with the *Cornus* varieties (dogwoods) providing the winter interest. For best effect the old stems need to be cut back each spring just beore the new growth begins. All the plants will require a humus–rich soil that does not dry out in the summer. Those plants that are actually bordering the stream will tolerate the soil being saturated throughout most of the year, but take care that the primulas are not submerged in water for more than a day or so following a wet spell, particularly in winter. Some shade provided by any nearby trees would be beneficial to some plants.

If the grass surrounds tend to be particularly wet in spring then *Fritillaria meleagris* and *Narcissus bulbocodium* may be freely planted in these areas. Where the gunneras still have their winter protection

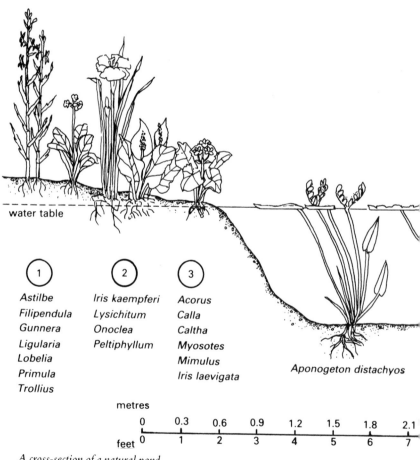

1

Astilbe
Filipendula
Gunnera
Ligularia
Lobelia
Primula
Trollius

2

Iris kaempferi
Lysichitum
Onoclea
Peltiphyllum

3

Acorus
Calla
Caltha
Myosotes
Mimulus
Iris laevigata

Aponogeton distachyos

metres

| 0 | 0.3 | 0.6 | 0.9 | 1.2 | 1.5 | 1.8 | 2.1 |

feet

| 0 | 1 | 2 | 3 | 4 | 5 | 6 | 7 |

A cross-section of a natural pond.

covering the crowns, the surrounding areas of damp soil provide a perfect situation for fritillarias to flower before the gunneras emerge in April – an idea cribbed from Christopher Lloyd of Great Dixter.

There could, of course, be many variations on the planting scheme that I have suggested. All depends on your own particular situation. Light woodland, for example, would lend itself more to informal plantings of primulas, astilbes and rodgersias rather than sun-loving plants. Certain kinds of ferns, too, would be ideal here.

I have not mentioned ferns before simply because the majority of

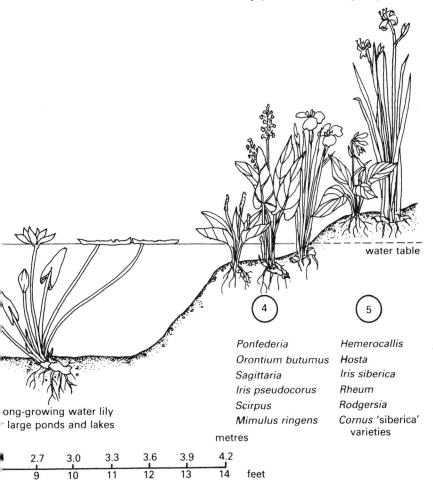

water table

(4) Ponfederia
Orontium butumus
Sagittaria
Iris pseudocorus
Scirpus
Mimulus ringens

(5) Hemerocallis
Hosta
Iris siberica
Rheum
Rodgersia
Cornus 'siberica'
varieties

ong-growing water lily
large ponds and lakes

metres

2.7	3.0	3.3	3.6	3.9	4.2	
9	10	11	12	13	14	feet

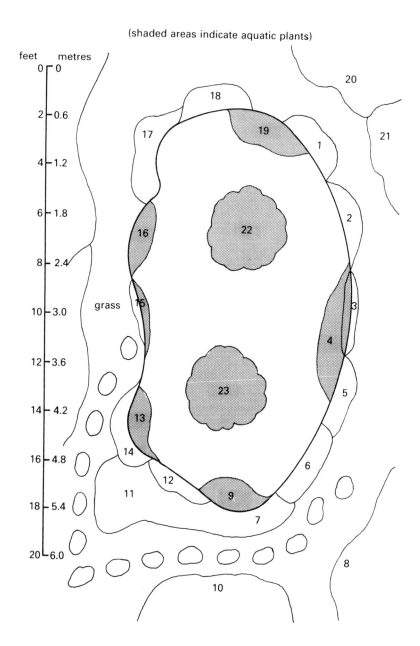

(shaded areas indicate aquatic plants)

A planting scheme for a water and bog garden.

them are shade-loving. However, there are a few that are well suited for most watery situations. *Osmunda regalis* (royal fern) requires a neutral-to-acid wet soil and some shade; it does not spread but sometimes reach 5–6ft (1.5–1.8m) in height. In autumn it turns to a beautiful colour, from rust to fox-red. *Struthiopteris germanica* (the shuttlecock fern), a handsome plant whose dramatic fresh-green fronds unfurl in spring, will, depending on the amount of moisture, reach 4–5ft (1.2–1.5m). *Onoclea sensibilis* (the sensitive fern) is so called on account of its sensitivity to autumn frosts, which will blacken the foliage instantly. Its creeping rootstock limits its value and it should be planted well away from other plants. Nevertheless, it is useful in the wilder parts of a damp woodland and for preventing the banks of a stream from slipping.

If this presents a problem, particularly with the wider and deeper streams or large natural ponds, drive stakes into the bank as illustrated, fix some rough boarding to the stakes and back-fill with soil so that nothing or at best very little is seen of the timbers. This will provide stability. Sometimes a path of some substance may be necessary to provide a walk. In an informal setting a path need only be made up by putting down rough ballast, such as Scalpings (granite chippings from Somerset). This is an excellent material and rarely needs any formal preparation such as would be needed for a more serviceable path. Informality is the key word when creating these natural water-garden features.

Plants for a Stream Garden

Key to Plan

1	*Caltha palustris*	(2–3)
2	*Leucojum aestivum* 'Gravetye Giant'	(6–7)
3	*Carex elata* (Bowles' golden sedge)	(3–4)
4	*Iris* × 'Gerald Derby'	(4–5)
5	*Lysichiton americanum*	(1)
6	*Primula denticulata*	(4–5)
7	*Iris pseudacorus* 'Variegatus'	(2–3)
8	*Primula rosea* 'Delight'	(4–5)
9	*Cornus alba* 'Aurea'	(1)
10	*Lobelia speciosa* 'Queen Victoria'	(4–5)
11	*Astilbe* 'White Gloria'	(3–4)
12	*Hemerocallis* 'Golden Chimes'	(3–4)
13	*Iris ochroleuca*	(2–3)
14	*Astilbe* 'Montgomery'	(3–4)

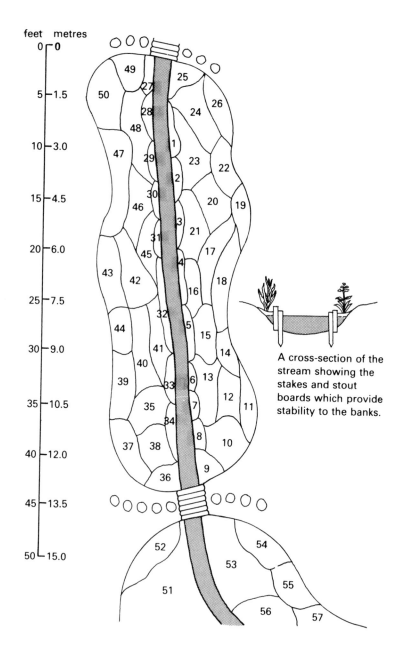

A cross-section of the stream showing the stakes and stout boards which provide stability to the banks.

The stream garden.

15	*Filipendula palmata*	(2–3)
16	*Trollius europaeus* 'Superba'	(4–5)
17	*Rodgersia aesculifolia*	(1–2)
18	*Hosta* 'Halcyon'	(3–4)
19	*Filipendula ulmaria* 'Aurea'	(2–3)
20	*Aconitum napellus* 'Bressingham Spire'	(3–4)
21	*Astilbe taquettii* 'Superba'	(3–4)
22	*Hemerocallis* 'Whichford'	(2–3)
23	*Lobelia speciosa* 'Will Scarlett'	(4–5)
24	*Iris kaempferi*	(3–4)
25	*Peltiphyllum peltatum*	(2–3)
26	*Trollius* 'Goldquelle'	(4–5)
27	*Myosotis scorpiodes (palustris)*	(2–3)
28	*Caltha palustris alba*	(4–5)
29	*Primula denticulata rubra*	(3–4)
30	*Caltha palustris plena*	(2–3)
31	*Lysichiton camtschatcense*	(1)
32	*Cornus alba* 'Kesselringii'	(1)
33	*Cardamine latifolia*	(3–4)
34	*Primula pulverulenta*	(3–4)
35	*Osmunda regalis*	(1–2)
36	*Aruncus sylvester (dioicus)*	(1)
37	*Astilbe* 'Serenade'	(2–3)
38	*Lythrum salicaria* 'Firecandle'	(2–3)
39	*Hosta fortunei* 'Aurea'	(3–4)
40	*Kirengeshoma palmata*	(2–3)
41	*Cimicifuga ramosa*	(3–4)
42	*Hemerocallis* 'Doubloon'	(2–3)
43	*Hosta* 'Thomas Hogg'	(2–3)
44	*Polygonum milletii*	(3–4)
45	*Lobelia vedrariensis*	(3–4)
46	*Ligularia przewalskii*	(2–3)
47	*Rodgersia podophyllum*	(2–3)
48	*Polygonum bistorta* 'Superbum'	(2–3)
49	*Polygonum amplexicaule* 'Atrosanguineum'	(2–3)
50	*Hosta sieboldiana* 'Elegans'	(1–2)
51	*Gunnera manicata*	(1)
52	*Primula japonica* 'Miller's Crimson'	(4–5)
53	*Primula helodoxa*	(4–5)
54	*Primula beesiana*	(4–5)
55	*Astilbe* 'Irrlicht'	(3–4)
56	*Cornus alba* 'Westonbirt'	(1)
57	*Primula pulverulenta* 'Bartley Strain'	(4–5)

9
THE WILDLIFE POOL

With the increasing awareness that the natural habitats of so many of our native species of flora and fauna are under constant threat of being destroyed by road, housing construction or other necessities of modern-day living, the term 'wildlife' has become significantly important. That is why I include a chapter describing very briefly the design of a wildlife pool and listing the species of plants that are most suitable.

Of all the particular kinds of wildlife gardening, none is more rewarding than the introduction of water into your own garden, however small your plot is. Not only do you introduce another range of plants that are suited only to such conditions, but numerous aquatic creatures soon colonize the water and any established pool will be teeming with such desirable amphibians as frogs, newts and toads and of course the creatures that spend their whole life in the water. It is important to remember not to introduce ornamental fish into a wildlife pond since they will eat young tadpoles, water beetles, water boatmen, pond skaters and so on. The most likely types of damselflies and dragonflies to visit a garden or wildlife pond in Britain are the blue-tailed damselfly, the common blue damselfly and, mainly in southern England, the broad-bodied chaser, the common hawker and the southern hawker dragonflies. These will breed in wildlife ponds.

A wildlife pond, like all others, should be sited in full sun and away from trees, particularly those which would cast shadows from the south or west. Leaves fall into a pond and build up poisonous gases which would, of course, be harmful to any of the hibernating creatures. To be at its most natural, the pool should be sited at the lowest part of the garden. The difference between creating a wildlife pond and a garden pond is that here we are imitating nature to the best of our ability, whereas with a garden pond it is the culture of water lilies and aquatics that takes precedence over everything else.

After deciding on the position of the pond the next step is to excavate and to construct pockets of various depths to accommodate the plants and amphibians. The size of the pond will, of course, depend on the area and size of the garden. The depth is important.

The pond should be at least 2ft (60cm) deep in the centre to prevent it freezing solid and to accommodate the hibernating creatures and the water lilies. *Nymphaea alba* (the native British white lily) might be too vigorous for the smaller wildlife pond. This depth reduces the problem of the formation of algae often the scourge of pools that are too shallow. The advantage of having a water lily in a wildlife pool – apart from the flowers – is that the leaves provide shade during hot weather for a number of creatures, and snails can lay eggs on the undersides of the leaves.

For lining the pool Butyl pool liner is considered the best material. It creates a more natural effect than either fibreglass or polythene.

I have never advocated the use of plastic planting containers for aquatics in garden ponds, and when it comes to planting up a wildlife pond nothing could be more incongruous than these grotesque containers showing through the water. For a really natural look the plants need to be planted directly into the soil so that in time many will merge with one another to provide the habitats for so many water creatures.

To achieve this effect, ideally you should excavate the site for the pool with sloping sides (garden pools generally have shelves for the various aquatics). The sloping sides of the pool will also provide access and escape routes for the amphibians. Some large stones or pebbles may be placed in the water extending over the ledge, while a rock or two forming a pocket for marginal plants will also provide a perch for birds. No definite shelves are found in pools or streams in the wild, so to prevent soil that is introduced to the pool from sinking to the bottom either make a ridge, using bricks for stability, or cut out a ridge if the soil is compact enough, so that the plants may be planted directly into the pool. Initially, plant each species in groups of two or three, depending on the size of the pool. For the planting medium use the same type of soil that is recommended for garden ponds. Wildlife pools need plenty of oxygenating plants to provide a haven for the many small creatures. The most suitable is *Ceratophyllum demersum*, hornwort. Simply drop the plants in; they will soon root and spread without becoming a nuisance.

For a beginner, a collection of aquatics easily obtainable from a nursery or garden centre would include *Sagittaria* (arrowheads), *Butomus umbellatus* (flowering rush), *Iris pseudacorus* (yellow flag iris), *Caltha palustris* (marsh marigold), *Stratiotes aloides* (water soldier) and, for the oxygenating plants, try *Ceratophyllum demersum* (hornwort) and *Callitriche stagnalis* (water starwort). These will give you a good start and more species may be added as the pool develops. Remembering never to collect the plants from the wild.

Those who have the good fortune to possess a river bank, a stream or even an old farm pond, now no longer used for its original purpose, have an advantage in that these offer scope to grow an unrivalled collection of bog and aquatic plants. In all probability some of the plants may already be established at the edge of a stream or river bank. The plants that you might expect to see in such positions would include *Rumex hydrolapathum* (great water dock), rising to 6ft or more (2m) with its long leaves, which assume such brilliant autumn colouring. Also close to the bank, in association with *Iris pseudacorus* you may find the true bulrush, *Scirpus lacustris*, with its striking dark-green cylindrical foliage. These plants are vigorous growers and will tolerate varying depths of water and current provided that they are well anchored initially until established.

Old farm ponds can make fine water features and usually have a wide margin of rich alluvial soil sloping gently towards the centre. This is ideal for rich plantings of numerous aquatics. *Butomus umbellatus* (flowering rush) associates well with *Myosotis palustris* (water forget-me-not). Water plantains (*Alisma* spp) produce fine flowering stems that remain in character right through the winter. Other native plants to consider for planting in bold masses beside lakes and large ponds are *Lysimachia vulgaris*, yellow loosestrife, and *Lythrum salicaria*, purple loosestrife. Plant these on the banks in damp or wet soil, but not in the water. These plants can, of course, be planted with confidence beside much smaller pools or on the banks of streams with an equally pleasing effect.

Plants for Shallow Water

Acorus calamus	sweet flag
Alisma plantago-aquatica	water plantain
Butomus umbellatus	flowering rush
Iris pseudacorus	yellow flag iris
Lemna spp	duckweed (floating plant)
Menyanthes trifoliata	bog bean
Myosotis palustris (scorpiodes)	water forget-me-not
Ranunculus lingua	greater spearwort
Rumex hydrolapathum	greater water dock
Sagittaria sagittifolia	arrowhead
Sparganium ramosum	bur-reed
Scirpus lacustris	true bulrush

Plants for Deep Water

Callitriche stagnalis	water starwort	(oxygenating plant)
Ceratophyllum demersum	hornwort	(oxygenating plant)
Hottonia palustris	water violet	(oxygenating plant)
Hydrocharis morsus-ranae	frog-bit	(floating plant)
	(This is also suited for growing in shallow pools)	
Myriophyllum spicatum	water milfoil	(oxygenating plant)
Nymphaea alba	white water lily	
Nuphar lutea	yellow water lily	
Nymphoides peltata	fringed water lily	
Potamogeton crispus	curled pondweed	(oxygenating plant)
Ranunculus aquatilis	water crowfoot	(oxygenating plant)
Stratiotes aloides	water soldier	(floating plant)

Plants for Bog and Marshy Areas Including the Banks of Streams

Caltha palustris	marsh marigold
Cardamine pratense	cuckoo flower
Cyperus longus	sweet garlingale
Filipendula ulmaria	meadowsweet
Geum rivale	water avens
Leucojum aestivum	summer snowflake
Lychnis flos-cuculi	ragged-robin
Lysimachia nummularia	creeping Jenny
Lysimachia vulgaris	yellow loosestrife
Lythrum salicaria	purple loosestrife
Menyanthes trifoliata	bog bean
Mentha aquatica	watermint
Mimulus guttatus	monkey flower
Myosotis palustris	water forget-me-not
Osmunda regalis	royal fern (for neutral-acid soil)
Veronica beccabunga	brook lime

PROTECTED PLANTS IN THE UNITED KINGDOM

All wild plants are protected by an Act of Parliament. The Wild Life and Countryside Act 1981 states that it is an offence to uproot

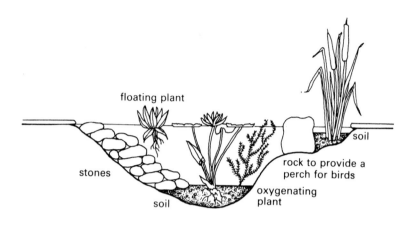

floating plant

soil

rock to provide a
perch for birds

stones

soil

oxygenating
plant

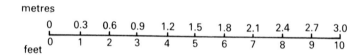

metres
0   0.3   0.6   0.9   1.2   1.5   1.8   2.1   2.4   2.7   3.0
0   1   2   3   4   5   6   7   8   9   10
feet

A cross-section of a wildlife pond showing the optimum depth.
If *Nymphaea alba* (the native British water lily) is difficult to
obtain or too vigorous for the smaller pond, then *N. × marlicea*
'Albida' is a very good substitute.
   Note the large stones placed at one side of the pool to provide
access or an escape route for some inhabitants. Generally
speaking, the larger the pool, the better. But the minimum size
that I consider most favourable for aquatics and water creatures
to thrive and live harmoniously together should be not less than
8×6ft (2.5×2m). Anything smaller could upset the balance of the
plant life and there would be too little room for the amphibians.

A cross-section of a wildlife pond using a butyl pool liner.

any wild plant, except under special circumstances, and it is also an
offence to collect seed from certain plants.

Further Reading

See *Creating a Wild Life Garden*, by Bob and Liz Gibbons (Hamlyn),
and *How to make a Wild Life Garden*, by C. Baines (Elm Tree
Books, London).

10
WATER GARDEN
CALENDAR

SEPTEMBER

Traditionally the gardener's year begins in the autumn, and in September the water garden will still have water lilies blooming. Some species of *Pontederia* may still be in flower but the cooler days will curtail the flowering of many aquatics now.

This is the time to remove fading blooms and spent foliage as too much left in the pond to rot in the autumn can cause problems later on with ornamental fish. You will probably also find that there is an entanglement of oxygenating plants, particularly *Elodea*. These, too, will need to be thinned out now.

The last of the perennial lobelias may be in flower, depending on the season, and ornamental grasses will still be in character. So will ferns of the *Osmunda* genus, which turn to a delightful golden brown as the autumn progresses and often remain so at least until Christmas. Astilbe flower heads that have faded hold some attraction during the autumn and can be left.

Towards the end of the month, cut back the leaves and old flower stems of waterside irises and other aquatics. Remove the spent material to the compost heap. The stems of *Scirpus* and *Typha* may look attractive if left throughout the autumn and winter but these make ideal hosts for various aquatic pests to overwinter on.

I have always favoured September as the month in which to lift and divide any large and congested clumps of *Caltha* (marsh marigold), particularly so with the single and double kinds. *Caltha palustris alba*, although slower growing, may also need dividing at this time. Trim back the foliage, which is often covered with mildew at this time of the year, and then replant in fresh soil. The plants soon settle in and will provide a reasonable show the following spring. If *Caltha polypetala* has outgrown its allotted space then it should be necessary only to cut back the spreading runners, and the foliage if it is looking a little untidy.

Echhornia crassipes (water hyacinth) must now be moved into a frost-free greenhouse and kept in a bowl containing soil and water until late May or after the danger of frost is over.

OCTOBER AND NOVEMBER

The first frosts will probably occur towards the end of the month, blackening any cannas that may have been grown in formal beds beside pools. These must be lifted, stored and treated like dahlias. Gunneras, too, will be scorched by the first frosts. This is the time to bend the uppermost leaves over the crowns and cover with straw or bracken.

Complete cutting back herbaceous plants that have finished flowering and tidy up the borders. Lobelias may be lifted and the clumps placed in a cold frame, or they may be left in the ground and covered with straw or bracken.

The early part of October is a good time to split and replant such perennials as astilbes, rodgersias and hostas. Most other plants are best divided in the spring.

One of the most oustanding displays in the water garden during October is *Cimicifuga ramosa*, thriving in any moisture-retentive soil. The pure-white bottle-brush-like flower heads on waving 6ft (2m) stems stand out in almost complete nakedness devoid of all competition from other plants, particularly if all the old flowering stems have been cut back and cleared away.

Callitriche verna will be prominent on the surface whilst *C. autumnalis* will be active below. Sometimes *Aponogeton distachyos*, the water hawthorn, will be flowering after a period of dormancy during the summer. *Hottonia palustris*, the water violet, springs into life by making a mass of pretty underwater foliage just when you think the plant had long since gone.

Autumn is an ideal time to plan and construct a garden pond. The completed pond will be filled with the natural rain of autumn and winter and you can avoid using tap-water, which tends to cause a build-up of lime scale on the liner. Do not, however, be tempted to plant any aquatics now. There is little chance of them surviving, particularly any bare-rooted material, and even container-grown plants give little advantage. Green water or algae will not be so much a problem at this time of year.

Netting spread over a small pool to prevent leaves being blown in is a practical idea.

WINTER

We can now enjoy the dramatic beauty of the dogwoods, which are so attractive beside water at this time of year.

Cornus alba 'Sibirica', the 'Westonbirt' dogwood, has the brightest red stems and is particularly effective growing in association with the greenish yellow stems of *Cornus stolonifera* 'Flavirinea' and the purple-black-stemmed *Cornus alba* 'Kesselringii'.

In the water, *Callitriche verna*, with its bright-green surface foliage, will be visible right through the winter months. In a mild January aponogetons have been seen flowering in sheltered ponds in the south of England.

If severe frosts are forecast, check that the gunneras are well protected and to prevent any straw or bracken from blowing away cover it with plastic netting and securely peg down.

Shallow pools such as tubs and sinks or very small prefabricated pools can be covered with boards and matting to prevent the ice penetrating the water lily crowns. Small bowls of young growing aquatics can be moved to a cold greenhouse.

Larger ponds, particularly where fish are present, must have an area free of ice. This acts as an escape route for poisonous gases, the by-products of decaying vegetation from aquatic growth in the pond. There are several ways to prevent ice forming and the one I favour is to place a short length of thick plank, free from creosote or wood preservative, in the pool before the onset of a severe frost. It is much easier to prevent a small area from freezing over than to break thick ice with a hammer or spade – which would anyway be disastrous for any fish. The shock waves stun the fish to death. Kettles of boiling water provide much the safest method of providing a small ice-free area for the benefit of ornamental fish.

Seeds of candelabra and drumstick primulas saved from the previous season may be sown now in a peat-based sowing compost or John Innes seed compost. Cover the seeds with a layer of fine grit. The trays or seed pans may be placed in a cold frame or outside to stratify, but be sure to protect them from cats and birds by placing some wire netting over them. Once germination has taken place, which is usually within 4–6 weeks, any boxes that have been outside can be brought in to a cold frame or greenhouse.

MARCH

Two months after Christmas and usually the worst of the winter is behind us, but as I write here in England we have just experienced the strongest storm force winds and flooding in living memory, bringing down thousands of trees and power lines and flooding hundreds of homes. Notwithstanding that traumatic experience, we have not had a frost since November. These very mild winters, of course, increase the risk of early infestations of greenfly, blackfly and hosts of other pests and diseases which would normally be killed off by winter frosts. It is easy for us to be lulled into a false sense of security for March can be a month of the unexpected. Winter sometimes arrives with a vengeance with sharp penetrating frosts damaging the early and often tender growths of many plants.

But in the water garden the marsh marigolds, the harbingers of spring, make a welcome appearance. Often the first to flower is the white version, *Caltha palustris alba*, followed by the giant marigold, *Caltha polypelata*, which has already produced an abundance of glossy green foliage, and by the end of the month our beautiful native *Caltha palustris* puts on its beautiful display of clear-yellow flowers. *Glyceria aquatica* 'Variegata' is now prominent with its young rose-purple shoots showing through the water. In favourable spring weather *Aponogeton distachyos* (water hawthorn) will be making a bold display with its scented white flowers. The earliest of the primulas to flower are the various strains of *Primula denticulata* (the drumstick primulas). They are guaranteed to give a good display in any moist bed or border, quickly followed by *Primula rosea* 'Delight' with its vivid carmine flowers. On the margins of the larger water garden the dramatic spathes of *Lysichiton* make their appearance.

Mild winter spells encourage the gunneras to force through their protective covering of leaves and straw and prematurely expose the frost-tender leaves. Any frost from now on would blacken the foliage, so protect the shoots at the first sign.

Choose a seasonably warm dry day to fork through the borders in the water garden, removing any weeds, especially any of the willow herbs, *Epilobium*. Then top-dress with well rotted compost or bark chippings. Overhauling the borders may also be tackled now, lifting overcrowded clumps of astilbes, hostas, rodgersias and the like and dividing and replanting them. Leave *Trollius* until after flowering. If extra stocks of lobelias and *Mimulus cardinalis* are required, then mid-March is the time for propagating them. First remove any straw used for winter protection and lift the clumps, divide them into the required number and pot into 3½in (8cm) pots and place in a cold frame. Freshly divided plants are subject to frost damage, so plant out during May.

It is still too early to consider planting any aquatics in the pool itself, no matter how sunny and warm the weather might be. The water will still be very cold. Much better to wait until next month.

In the nursery, small divisions of such aquatics as *Myosotis palustris*, *Veronica beccabunga*, *Glyceria aquatica* 'Variegata', *Mentha aquatica*, *Mimulus luteus*, *Mimulus ringens* are lifted from the outside stock ponds and potted into 3½in pots, using a straight loam. These are then placed in a water tray and grown on under cold glass or a poly-tunnel. They should, of course, be hardened off before being offered for sale to the public, so expect to see them in nurseries and garden centres from mid-April onwards. If you are ordering your aquatic plants from a mail order nursery, send off your order without delay and expect to receive the plants by late April or early May.

APRIL

This month the water will slowly begin to warm up, encouraging aquatic plants to make visible signs of spring growth. Already *Caltha* (marsh marigolds) are making their bold displays of bright yellow. The *Lysichiton* species, too, with their yellow or white spathes make a dramatic show at the pond or stream side. But April can be a very precarious month weather-wise. Some of the most damaging frosts of the winter can occur. This seems particularly so if the winter has been exceptionally mild, encouraging early growths of most plants to flower several weeks earlier than usual. But of course even temperatures falling to as low as 21°F (−6°C), which is not uncommon in the Midlands and the North, will damage the foliage and flowers only and not the rootstock. Nevertheless, it is enough to spoil the blooms for that season.

April is the busiest month of the year for most gardeners, not excluding the water gardener. During showery spells many waterside plants not divided and replanted last month may still be planted now. In the garden centre, pot-grown aquatic plants will be making their appearance by the middle of the month. Unfortunately, though, many may have been brought on under cold glass or polythene tunnels at the nursery and not hardened off, thus making them susceptible to any sudden change in temperature. Aquatics purchased in 3½in pots will need to be potted on into 2-litre aquatic baskets or into properly constructed pockets within the pools, using good garden loam. Water lilies established in aquatic containers will of course be safe to move now. But do not expect any aquatic plants that have been ordered by mail order to be delivered before early May. This is quite soon enough to plant bare-root material – in fact, May is the best month by far.

Easter is traditionally the time for cleaning out and replanting overgrown ponds, assuming that Easter falls around the middle of April. This will apply particularly to the smaller pool where the lilies and aquatic plants have outgrown their containers. Their life in these is normally three or four years. If a complete clean-out is contemplated, any fish present will need to be moved into temporary quarters. In larger ponds it will be a matter of thinning out overgrown pockets of marginal plants and reducing excess amounts of oxygenating plants. This is a good time to remove any algae before it becomes entangled with the new growth of the water lilies and other aquatic plants, and of course any remaining dead leaves from the winter that were not removed earlier. This particularly applies to the smaller pool, where too much decaying vegetation would be harmful to any fish present.

By this month the dogwoods (*Cornus alba* 'Sibirica' and its varieties) will be beginning to burst into leaf. These should now be cut back hard to encourage new stems for the following winter, since these always produce the best colour for winter effect. It may not always be necessary to prune annually; every second year may be sufficient.

One of the most spectacular of all ornamental grasses that is in character now is *Carex elata* 'Aurea' (Bowles' golden sedge). Growing best in a damp situation and in full sun, the rough arching foliage is a golden-yellow but in damp shade the colour is a soft lime-green. This sedge is at its best this month and next.

In the pool itself the *Aponogeton* will still be making a reasonable show, which often starts in early March in favourable seasons. Many waterside plants will now be in character. The summer snowflake, *Leucojum aestivum* 'Gravetye Form', makes a delightful contrast to the calthas, while the intense-carmine *Primula rosea* 'Delight' together with *P. denticulata* look superb at the edge of any damp spot, near water but not actually in the water itself. The giant saxifrage *Peltiphyllum peltatum*, useful for keeping the banks of streams in place with its tough creeping rootstock, produces its naked 2ft (60cm) stems with round heads of starry-pink flowers.

Osmunda regalis (royal fern), which is only suitable for an acid peaty soil, will be unfurling its delicate olive-green fronds by the end of the month.

MAY

This is the month for planting all aquatics; there is no other time in the year that is quite so ideal. This is because the days are lengthening (whatever the weather), and the temperature of the water is increasing, which encourages the growth of the aquatics and water lilies. Growth is not so far advanced that planting causes any undue setback. This is also the busiest month in the aquatic nursery, where all mail orders will be despatched, or in the garden centres, where the container-grown stock will be looking its best. When choosing water lilies (*Nymphaea* spp), select if possible those that are growing in the open-weave type of container, that is if you intend to continue growing them in containers. If, however, they are in 'solid' containers, you will need either to transfer them direct to the soil at the bottom of the pool or replant them in an open-weave-type basket. This is because the strong roots will need the freedom to grow outside the confines of the pot and this type of basket also allows the exchange of the various gases to take place.

You may see the perennial *Lobelia fulgens hybrida* often but erroneously labelled 'Cardinalis' offered as a plant to grow in the garden pool. It will probably thrive for a season but thereafter it will rot away. Far better to plant this in a damp border beside the pool where it will be perennial.

Seedlings and cuttings of lobelias made earlier can be moved out of the frames or greenhouse to harden off ready to plant out later in the month. The primulas, too, can be moved outside, but protect them from strong sunlight with suitable netting or place the trays of seedlings against the north side of a building. Towards the end of the month or early in June the seedlings should be large enough to be either potted up singly into 3in pots or turned out into prepared nursery beds. Water well in and keep shaded.

A complete overhaul of an established pool can be made now; there will be no better time. Any replanted lilies and aquatics will soon settle into fresh growing conditions and should provide a reasonable display by July or August.

So far I have mentioned only the work that needs to be done this month. What to expect to be flowering at this time in the water garden can vary according to the season and local conditions.

Experience has shown that plants flower some 3–4 weeks later in the north of England than in the south.

Quite often *Caltha palustris* (marsh marigold) will still be making a show long after the double variety has finished. But then to follow the calthas is the reliable *Orontium aquaticum* (golden club), another yellow-flowered aquatic. A very long-lived plant that never becomes a nuisance, it does need a deep soil to do well. The rushes (*Scirpus* spp) will be sending up their attractive variegated stems sometimes inches each day depending on the temperature. But rarely do the *Nymphaea* (water lilies) show any blooms this month; you will have to wait until early June even for well established plants. *Hydrocharis morsus-ranae* (frog-bit) will begin to show signs of growth as the dormant winter buds come out of their resting state and surface. And any *Nymphaea* seeds sown late last summer will begin to germinate and show signs of growth – but keep the containers or bowls in which they are growing still under glass and keep the water level to about 2–3in (5–7cm) to ensure that no snails are present, since these will quickly devour the young plants.

In the bog garden and damp borders the hostas are in pristine condition, provided that the slugs have not attacked them. The gunneras develop their enormous leaves and will be particularly good as the summer advances if they have been well mulched and fed in April. The rheums, too, in their various forms, spread their stately foliage, but remember that these do not require so much moisture as the gunneras.

Often in the larger water garden where these particular plants flourish the background in the form of trees provides light shade, and this is preferred. It is the water lilies that like to be in full sun. Other waterside plants that prefer light shade, and are in character this month, are *Iris pseudacorus* and its variety *I. p.* 'Variegata'. Also waterside ferns – *Osmunda regalis*, *Struthiopteris germanica* and *Onoclea sensibilis* – are of interest, though the last two can become a nuisance by their spreading root system. They do, however, provide the perfect foil for the candelabra primulas which will give such a wealth of colour this month.

JUNE

June is the month for irises – *I. laevigata*, *I. kaempferi* and the other waterside species which make their display without fail. It is midsummer and many other aquatics and waterside plants too numerous to list will be in character now. The water lilies will begin to bloom and will continue to flower right through to the end of September. 'Escarboucle' is one variety that often gives the longest display. Although each individual bloom lasts five to six days, it will continue to produce buds right through the summer. Everything should now be looking at its best, with the lush growth of the waterside plants enhancing the beauty of the garden pool. The exceptions are of course the informal pools, where the surroundings will be either paving of one sort or another, and the symmetrical pool set in the lawn where any sort of additional planting would look out of place.

Whatever the type of pool, now is the time to keep a lookout for any pest that may occur. If the water lily beetle is known to exist from a previous season the grubs will now be seen on the lily pads. One way to deal with them is to use strong jet from a hosepipe to dislodge them into the water. Any fish present will devour them as part of their normal diet. Action now will prevent a build-up to possible epidemic proportions later on in the season. Iris sawfly and aphids could also be present at this time, so take the necessary action at the first signs of trouble.

June is an excellent month to plant all aquatics. The late starters, *pygmaea* water lilies for example, will be making good growth to both leaves and roots so that transplanting now will present no real setback. In fact *pygmaea* lilies purchased as 'loose' from a mail order nursery will begin to flower within six weeks or so. The tiny floating plant *Hydrocharis morsus-ranae* (frog-bit) will be fully grown from the winter buds that surfaced towards the end of last month.

If you sowed water lily seeds last summer or autumn they should have germinated by April. Once germinated, I prefer to leave them in the bowl until they are well established, then carefully lift them out and pot them on individually in 3in pots and stand them in a bowl or bowls of water. Alternatively, if the seeds were sown individually in glass or plastic phials, then transplanting can take place that much earlier.

The offsets or eyes of lilies taken last summer and rooted in bowls of loam and water will also have made sufficient growth to enable them to be transplanted into pools of shallow water to begin with, gradually topping up as the growth increases.

In natural ponds and also in wildlife ponds, some of the plants introduced may be of a more vigorous nature, so some thinning out may be necessary to prevent the feature from becoming completely obliterated and the water hidden from view by the sheer mass of vegetation.

In all ponds, both new and established, where algae (blanketweed) can present a problem, there is really only one way to get rid of this nuisance, and that is to remove it by hand or with a garden rake. I have never recommended the use of any chemicals.

You may notice that some water lily leaves will have had some semicircular pieces taken out. If you turn the leaf over you will find the missing piece fixed to the underside of the leaf. Within this capsule will be found the grub of the brown china-mark moth. These really need destroying, but do try to avoid the use of chemicals. Dislodge the grubs so that either the fish can devour them or they can be just picked off if that is at all practical.

This month is ideal for introducing ornamental fish to a pond, particularly if it was planted during late April or early May. Those few weeks will allow enough time for the plants to settle in before the introduction of the fish. If the fish are introduced any sooner, they will want to investigate their new surroundings by nosing into the mud and will tend to dislodge the plants. Always buy the smallest size available, 2–3in (5–7cm); at this size they will travel satisfactorily without too much stress and will soon settle in their new surroundings. Avoid buying fish during very hot sultry weather or during thundery spells.

JULY

At the height of the summer the water garden will be at its best. Water lilies planted in May will begin to flower this month, but those that are established will of course be at their best now. *Hemerocallis* and *Filipendula* (meadowsweet) will be making a colourful display in any damp border. However, some varieties of *Filipendula* are subject to an attack of mildew now. Should this happen, trim the foliage to ground level and new growth will soon appear. *F. u. aurea* is particularly vulnerable to attack.

Nothing surpasses the brilliance of the astilbes or their many subtle shades and diversity of form, from the dwarf *simplicifolia* hybrids to the tall majestic *arendsii* and *davidii* varieties. They are unrivalled in the damp border and are in character this month and for much of the next.

Keep an eye open for any undesirable pests attacking the water lilies, in particular the water lily beetle if it is known to exist from past seasons. This creature was mentioned for June, as it is one of the most devastating of all aquatic pests. Early action is by far the best way of eradicating it. Aphids can be a problem too. If you have fish in the pond, dislodge the aphids with the aid of a jet from a hose so that the fish can feed on them.

Seeds of *Orontium aquaticum* will be ripening now and next month. As they are the size of peas they can be sown individually into 3in pots and placed in bowls of water. They will be ready to plant out the following spring. The pods of *Aponogeton distachyos* can be placed in a bowl containing soil and an inch of so of water, where germination will take place within a few weeks.

Sometimes blanketweed (algae) appears for no apparent reason. It is always best to remove it there and then before it becomes a long-drawn-out task, particularly in the larger pool. A narrow moss rake or springbok is an ideal tool for pulling it out between lily leaves. Before consigning it to the compost heap, make sure that no ramshorn snails or young fish have been caught in the thick strands of the algae.

Above all, enjoy the water garden now and next month, for it can be one of the most desirable features in your garden, whether it is in miniature or a large expanse of water.

AUGUST

The feature plant for the water garden this month must surely be the perennial lobelia. *L. speciosa* 'Queen Victoria' and its numerous varieties. All make a dramatic show of colour as a waterside plant (never plant them in the water itself as they will only rot away after flowering).

Gunnera manicata will be at its greatest size right now. It is a plant for the really large water garden, where it will be an imposing feature and it is of immense architectural value.

Seeds of most primulas should be ready for collecting now. They can either be sown right away in pans or trays with a standard seed compost and placed in a frame shaded from the sun, or sown in January, when they can be stratified before germination takes place. *P. helodoxa* seed is best sown as soon as ripe, since germination will be very patchy if it is left until the spring. *Iris kaempferi* and *I. laevigata* seed pods should also be ready for collecting but leave the sowing until the following spring; February–March is quite soon enough for these.

If you are on holiday this month, and your holiday includes visiting other people's gardens open to the public, this could provide an opportunity to make a few notes on some established water gardens for future reference. It could give you ideas for adjustments to make to your own garden or stimulate any plans you might have for the construction of a pond or the design of a water garden feature over the winter ready for planting during the following spring. Visits could include aquatic nurseries. This is a quiet period for them and you would see many varieties in full bloom, and of course many other aquatics. The staff should be able to give you some sound advice should you require it. You could even buy any particular plant that appeals to you if it is in a container – that is, of course, assuming that you already have a pool. So why wait until next spring? Planting any loose (not in pots) marginal plants now could be risky as they may not be sufficiently well established before the autumn and winter. Bare-rooted water lilies, however, can be safely transplanted this month. In fact, this is what the aquatic nurseries will be doing now – potting up water lilies in aquatic containers for overwintering. These will then be well established by next April.

It is never worth planting aquatics after the end of August because the cooler temperatures and shorter daylight hours limit the time for establishment before the onset of the autumn.

APPENDICES

I WHERE TO SEE WATER LILIES

United Kingdom

The National Collection of Hardy Water Lilies is held at Burnby Hall Garden, Pocklington, North Yorkshire (14 miles (23km) east of York). The Gardens are open throughout the summer months. The collection was first established in the 1930s by Major Stewart and now, with over fifty varieties established, is managed by Stapely Water Garden, Nantwich. The nomenclature and all scientific research and recording is undertaken by Wycliffe Hall Botanic Garden, Barnard Castle.

The Royal Horticultural Society Garden at Wisley has a display of named varieties of water lilies established in an informal pool in front of the society's offices and laboratory.

Further south, in Dorset, is Bennett's Water Lily Farm at Chickerell, Weymouth, where a wide range of water lilies can be seen growing in a natural setting.

Nurseries specializing in water lilies and aquatic and waterside plants

Bennett's Water Lily Farm,
Putton Lane,
Chickerell,
Weymouth,
Dorset DT3 4AF.

Higher End Nursery,
Hale,
Fordingbridge,
Hampshire SP6 2RA.

Longstock Park Nursery,
Longstock,
Hampshire SO20 6EH.

J. M. Smith,
The Water Garden Nursery,
Highcroft,
Moorend,
Wembworthy,
Chulmleigh,
Devon EX18 7SG.

Honeysome Aquatic Nursery,
The Row,
Sutton,
Near Ely,
Cambridgeshire CB6 2PF.

Wychwood Carp Farm,
Farnham Road,
Odiham,
Near Basingstoke,
Hampshire RG25 1HS.

Australia

Gedye Water Gardens,
37–41 Elizabeth Street,
Doncaster East,
3109 Victoria.

An old established aquatic nursery where *Nymphaea* 'Norma Gedye' was raised.

Federal Republic of Germany

Karl Wachter,
Rollbarg,
D-2081 Appen-Etz.

A general nursery and garden centre, but regards aquatics as an important part of the nursery business.

Dettmar Moller,
Cuxhavener Strasse 577,
D-2104 Hamburg.

Has a small nursery which grows and retails aquatics. A visit is recommended.

Junge,
Seerosen,
D-3250 Hamlin.

This is a large, old and well-established aquatic nursery where *Nymphaea* 'Rosennymphe' was raised in 1911.

Jorg Petrowsky,
Hermannsburger Strasse 42,
D-3106 Echede.

Water lilies growing in many lakes are to be seen here.

Walter Radloff,
Schnieglinger Strasse 54,
D-8500 Nurenburg 90.
An aquatic nursery specializing in uncommon bog and marginal plants.

Munich Botanical Gardens,
Munich.
Displays a good collection of hardy water lilies and aquatic plants.

France

Establishment Latour Marliac,
Le Temple-sur-Lot 47100.
This is where Joseph Bory Latour Marliac raised most of the hardy varieties of water lilies that are grown in gardens today. Although he died in 1911, the nursery is still in business and is now owned by two great-grandsons of the founder, Phillipe and Henri Laydeker, but managed by M. Guy Maurel. Many varieties are grown in the original concrete ponds which have all been repaired during the last few years, and the nursery is now in a condition as Marliac would have left it in 1911. A price list is available and orders are dealt with by post. However, anyone contemplating a visit would be well advised to acquaint themselves with the French language as the staff speak no English.

Claude Monet's garden at Giverny, near Vernon which is about fifty miles north-west of Paris has become a place of pilgrimage for garden lovers from all over Europe. The Japanese too, find the gardens irresistible. This celebrated water garden with its wisteria-clad Japanese bridge has been restored to its former glory, just as Monet would have left it in 1926. The gardens are now in the care of Academie des Beaux-Arts.

New Zealand

Wirihana Tropicals,
Lindsay Road,
RD9, Frankton,
North Island.
A nursery growing both hardy and tropical water lilies.

South Africa

Lovemore Plants,
PO Box 72098,
Parkview 2122,
Johannesburg.
   This nursery has published an excellent handbook on pond plants. Although written for South Africa it would be of value to anyone interested in aquatics.

United States of America

Denver Botanic Gardens,
Denver,
Colorado.
   Displays an unrivalled collection of hardy water lilies, all of which are labelled to botanic garden standards.
   The water garden at Denver Botanic Gardens was established in 1959, but over the years it had become neglected and little used. In 1981 however, Joe Tomocik, a former school master was employed by the Botanic Garden to restore and develop the Water Garden. Due to Joe Tomocik's enthusiasm the pools now display one of the most comprehensive collections or hardy and tropical water lilies in the United States.
   After two years with the Denver Botanical Garden, Joe Tomocik offered a beginner's course on water gardening. Such was the enthusiasm at the inaugural meeting that a nucleus of 10 people formed the Colorado Water Garden Society in 1983. The Society now has 200 members and holds six meetings a year with additional related activities including tours of members' gardens in July.

Lilypons Water Gardens,
6800 Lilypons Road,
PO Box 10,
Buckeystown,
Maryland 21717-0010.
   This is a family-run business, established many years ago and now offering a useful range of hardy water lilies including some tropical forms. This firm also has a recently established branch in Texas (PO Box 188, Brookshire). Excellent catalogues are available from both nurseries.

Longwood Gardens,
Kennett Square,
Near Philadelphia,
Pennsylvania.

Both hardy and tropical water lilies are grown to perfection in these gardens, which were established in 1957 and are now greatly improved. Seeds of the Longwood strain of *Victoria regia* are sent to botanical gardens throughout the world including the Royal Botanic Gardens at Kew.

Perry's Water Garden,
191 Leatherman Gap Road,
Franklin,
North Carolina.

Perry Slocum, who founded the Slocum's Water Gardens in 1939, established these gardens on his retirement in 1980. The best of the hardy water lilies flower in profusion and he has also raised many new varieties.

Slocum's Water Garden,
1101 Cypress Gardens Road,
Winter Haven,
Florida 33880.

This nursery is now run by Perry Slocum's son, Peter. Tropical lilies are to be seen growing outside under natural conditions. An excellent catalogue is available offering hardy and tropical water lilies.

Missouri Botanic Gardens,
St Louis.

George Pring produced many excellent tropical hybrid water lilies here, including the well known 'General Pershing' in 1917. Several outdoor ponds display many of Pring's hybrids.

The National Arboretum,
Washington DC.

The main administrative buildings are surrounded by water where a fine collection of both hardy and tropical water lilies are grown. All are named and a visit is recommended.

As with almost all other genera of hardy plants there is a society to promote knowledge of the science and culture of water lilies and aquatic plants. The International Water Lily Society was founded in 1984 and now has over 600 members in 23 countries with its headquarters at South West Texas State University, San Marcos, TX 78666, USA. Membership of the Society includes a subscription to the *Water Garden Journal* which is published quarterly. For membership details write to:

The European Treasurer,
International Water Lily Society,
19 Putton Lane,
Weymouth,
Dorset DT3 4AF,
United Kingdom.

II GLOSSARY OF BOTANICAL TERMS

Adventitious roots Roots growing in abnormal places, for example from nodes on the stem of the plant.

Adventitious shoots Shoots growing in abnormal places, for example from internodal parts of the plant and basal suckering.

Anther Part of a stamen that carries the pollen.

Axis The main stem of a plant.

Biternate A leaf consisting of two leaflets; two leaves in opposition round a common axis.

Calyx The outer whorl of floral leaves. The sepals are usually green.

Contiguous So close as to touch one another.

Convulate Rolled together, or over each other.

Cordate Heart-shaped leaves.

Corolla The inner whorl of petals; divisions of a flower within the calyx.

Dentate The margins of a leaf are divided into tooth-like incisions.

Dioscorides A native of Anazauba in Cilicia, Turkey, who lived at the time of Nero. His celebrated book on medicinal herbs was the foundation of most botanical knowledge until modern times.

Eye A dormant bud attached to a tuber or rhizome.

Farinose Mealy, having the texture of flour on some stems and leaves.

Fasciation When a stem or branches become flattened from a single stem, or a number of stems are merged into a single fasciated structure. Where a *Nymphaea* rootstock and crown becomes flattened due to fasciation it fails to produce any buds or flowers.

Glabrous Smooth, without hairs.

Globose   Round or spherical-shaped.

Genus   A group of plants having common structural characteristics distinct from those of all other groups.

Hastate   Spear-shaped leaves.

Hydrophytes   A plant that grows in water.

Habit   The general form of the plant.

Inflorescence   The flower cluster.

Involute   The leaves whose edges are rolled inwards.

Lanceolate   Lance-shaped leaves.

Linear   Narrow and with the two sides almost parallel.

Node   The part of a stem from which a leaf arises.

Obovate   Egg-shaped leaf with the broadest end uppermost.

Offset   A short lateral stem ending in a compact lateral shoot which on detachment may form a new plant vegetatively reproduced.

Order   The natural order or plant family.

Palmate   The leaves are lobed in the shape of a hand palm with a rib radiating to each lobe.

Panicle   The flowerhead or inflorescence having the axis divided into branches bearing two or more flowers.

Pedicel   The stem or support of a single flower; the final branch of the inflorescence.

Peltate   shield-like. The petiole of a peltate leaf is attached to the lower surface instead of to the margin.

Pericarp   The shell of fruit formed from the ripened ovary wall.

Petiole   The stalk of a leaf.

Procumbent   Plants lying flat on the ground.

Pubescent   Covered with soft downy hairs.

Pliny (*The Elder*, AD 23–79)   Roman writer and naturalist.

Raceme   An inflorescence in which the flowers are arranged singly on distinct pedicels along a common stem or axis.

Rhizome   An underground 'rootstock', usually horizontal, sending up flowering stems and leaves.

Sagittate   Arrow-shaped leaves.

Sepals   A leaf of a calyx or the outermost whorl of a flower. The sepals are usually green and unlike the petals.

Sessile   A flower attached to a stem without any stalk.

Sinus   The space formed between the lobes of a leaf, as with the leaves of a water lily.

Spadix   A fleshy spike usually enclosed before flowering in one or more spathes, especially in *Aroides*.

Spathe   A bract situated on the flower stalk below the inflorescence and surrounding the latter until the flowers are ready to open.

Species   The individual plants of similar genetical constitution that are seed-raised from a common parent. They may differ from each other in colour of the flower, size of leaf, and so on. Crosses between different species are usually infertile.

Spike   An inflorescence in which the flowers are sessile along an undivided stem or axis.

Stolon   An elongated shoot arising from the base of the parent stem and rooting at the tip, forming a new plant. Examples are *Ranunculus lingua* and *Sagittaria* spp.

Theophrastus (circa 373–287 BC)   Succeeded Aristotle as President of the Lyceum at Athens. His *History of Plants* and *Moral Characters* are the best-known of his writings.

Tomentose   Thickly pubescent.

Umbel   An inflorescence in which the flowers expand from stalks that radiate from a common centre.

Ventricose   Swelling unequally or inflated on one side.

Villose   Shaggy, covered with long and soft hairs.

Whorl   A ring of flowers or leaves at one node surrounding the stem or axis.

Xerophytic   A plant that can flourish in hot and dry conditions or under conditions of poor water supply.

III   BIBLIOGRAPHY

Bloom, Alan,   *Moisture Gardening* (Faber & Faber, 1966).

Coulter, Barnes Cowles,   *Text Book of Botany* (American Book Company, 1911).

Farrer, Reginald,   *Alpines and Bog Plants* (Arnold, 1908).

Jekyll, Gertrude,   *Wall and Water Gardens* (George Newnes, 1902).

Journals of the International Water Lily Society, 1987–.

Nicholson, George,   *The Illustrated Dictionary of Gardening*.

Perry, Amos,   *Water Plants* (*circa* 1930).

Perry, Frances,   *Water Gardening* (*Country Life*, 1961).

Perry, Frances,   *Water Gardens* (Penguin, 1962).

Robinson, William,   *The English Flower Garden* (John Murray, eighth edn, 1903).

Royal Horticultural Society, *Dictionary of Gardening* (Clarendon Press, Oxford, 1951).

Thomas, Graham Stuart,   *Perennial Garden Plants* (Dent, 1976).

Trehane, Piers,.   *Index Hortensis* (Quarterjack Publishing, Wimborne, 1989).

INDEX